D0833954

The Lost Art of Pot et Fleur

FLOWER ARRANGING

— WITH —

HOUSE PLANTS

The Lost Art of Pot et Fleur

FLOWER ARRANGING
—WITH—
HOUSE PLANTS

SUSAN CONDER

Photography by Marie-Louise Avery

BOXTREE

DEDICATED TO NAOMI L. HELLER, MY MOTHER

First published in Great Britain in 1995 by Boxtree Limited

Conceived and produced by Breslich & Foss, London

Volume copyright © Breslich & Foss 1995
Text copyright © Susan Conder 1995

The right of Susan Conder to be identified as Author of this Work has been
asserted by her in accordance with the Copyright Designs and Patents Act 1988.

1 3 5 7 9 10 8 6 4 2

All rights reserved. Except for use in a review, no part of this book may be
reproduced, stored in a retrieval system or transmitted in any form or by any
means, electronic, mechanical, photocopying, recording or otherwise, without prior
permission of Boxtree Limited.

Photography by Marie-Louise Avery
Photographs on pages 1, 47, 50 and 85 by Sue Atkinson
The extracts from *Flower Decoration in the House* by Gertrude Jekyll on pages
8 and 9 appear by kind permission of the Antique Collector's Club
Designed by Nigel Partridge

Printed and bound in Italy

Produced by Breslich & Foss for
Boxtree Limited
Broadwall House
21 Broadwall
London SE1 9PL

A CIP Catalogue entry for this book is available from the British Library

ISBN 07522 1633 3

Jacket photography by Marie-Louise Avery

CONTENTS

❖ ❖ ❖

INTRODUCTION

❖ ❖ ❖

RIGHT A pot et fleur in progress – small, sun-like *senecio* flowers provide an excellent 'filler' for maidenhair ferns, yellow variegated ivy and mop-headed African marigolds.

The term 'pot et fleur', French for pot and flower, was in fact first used in England in 1960, in response to an article in *The Daily Telegraph* by Violet Stevenson. The article discussed mixing cut flowers and house plants, with the former providing ever-changing, short-term seasonal colour and interest, and the latter, an ongoing background.

The art of combining cut flowers, foliage and house plants to create indoor displays goes back, however, to the Victorian era. Though in the eighteenth century the rich grew exotic plants in their conservatories, it was not until the nineteenth century that the penchant for decorative house plants and cut flowers gained favour. The British annexation of India, where flowers and lavish floral decoration were much in evidence in daily life, may have influenced this new fashion, and the rapid growth of cities and solid, stolid suburbs, with relatively small or absent gardens, meant that both flowering and foliage house plants took on added value.

In Victorian England, and in nineteenth-century Australia and America where culture and fashion were still strongly influenced by England, epergnes were considered essential for pot et fleur displays. These tiered, often branched, table-centre ornaments, filled with potted maidenhair ferns, ivy garlands, cut flowers and fresh fruit, graced fashionable dining tables, sideboards and entrance halls.

The quest for impressive pot et fleurs reached the limits of absurdity, to the detriment of the furniture and dinner guests, when holes were actually cut in antique tables and fine damask tablecloths to hide the flowerpots and cross-table conversation was made impossible by the sheer height and breadth of the displays. The winning display of the pot et fleur class at the 1872 Royal Horticultural Society exhibition comprised:

...two large ferns let into the table, and surrounded by fern leaves, so as to hide all appearance of their being done. The centrepiece was singularly elegant – a tall glass, with Cacti blooms at the base of it; the vase itself containing Lily of the Valley, salmon-coloured Geraniums and light Grasses. On either side were two recumbent figures surrounded by moss...

THE JOURNAL OF HORTICULTURE, 1872

Eventually, fashions changed and in 1907 the gardening writer and designer Gertrude Jekyll wrote:

The greater number of table centrepieces made during the middle reign of Queen Victoria are not now sources of pride to their owners. There was a favourite pattern of camels and palm trees that was reproduced by the hundred – a notable example of the depths to which the silversmith's art could sink. At the same time there were pretentious articles of silver gilt and gilt brass with hanging glass dishes, such as, in our more enlightened days, could not appear upon a good table. So much for the Victorian epergne.

FLOWER DECORATION IN THE HOUSE, GERTRUDE JEKYLL (COUNTRY LIFE/GEORGE NEWNES LTD, 1907, ANTIQUE COLLECTOR'S CLUB, 1982)

In 1950, Violet Stevenson reiterated that disapproval:

Not only did it fall to the Victorians to reintroduce the custom of using flowers, but it fell to them also to bring into use many of the most unsuitable containers in which to place them. Worst of all, it fell to them to discover the epergnes. They filled them with flowers and fruit looking like Harvest Festivals or frozen fountains; either towering up so that you viewed your neighbour from beneath a banner of flowers, or spreading down the centre of the table until it became a decorated table instead of a table decoration.

FLOWER DECORATION FOR THE HOME, VIOLET STEVENSON, (COLLINGRIDGE, 1950)

Both authors, however, recognised that combining cut flowers and house plants was an exciting concept, full of potential, and a simplified form found favour with both writers. Gertrude Jekyll, for example, wrote in the same book in which she disparaged epergnes:

> ...the cut Orchid of largely branching habit may be with advantage grouped with the whole fern growing in a pot. The natural disposition of the fronds of growing ferns is so good that it is difficult to imitate with any artificial arrangement of them cut; besides, cut fern fronds do not live long in water, even if they have had the preparatory overhead soaking...

❖

Contemporary Adaptations

Displays can be formal or informal with endless permutations. Options range from creating an indoor garden of several different foliage house plants in a large container, with flowers incorporated, to a display based on a single specimen house plant. Flowering house plants can be given a 'ruffle' of cut garden foliage such as variegated periwinkle or velvety grey *Senecio*, which, tucked round the rim of a cachepot, gives an instant, sophisticated effect. Cut and growing flowers can be combined: a huge basket filled with blue and white, daisy-like cineraria house plants, for example, plus blue and white cornflowers, ageratum and white roses.

As well as combining cut and growing material in the same container, 'communal' pot et fleur displays can be created – for example, a ring of small terracotta pots filled with velvety mind-your-own-business or creeping moss, set around a central glass goblet of mixed spring flowers or a tightly packed bunch of lilies-of-the-valley.

The approach is eminently practical and economic, since long-term foliage house plants can be re-used for months or even years and silk, dried and glycerined flowers and foliage can add variety, especially in winter. Ranging from the simple to the extravagant, pot et fleur is an invitation to be creative and to look at nature's raw material in a new light.

CONTAINERS

❖ ❖ ❖

A pot et fleur container can combine the flamboyance of a vase with the practicality of a flower pot, and match its contents in beauty or play a subtle, supporting role.

❖

INNER CONTAINERS AND SUPPORTS

A traditional pot et fleur consists of an outer container containing one or more house plants plus cut material which can be contained in and supported by any of the following: saturated florist's foam packed into the outer container; a shallow, water-filled bowl with a metal pinholder; or a water-filled glass, plastic or metal tube sunk into the potting compost. Dried flowers, seedpods, glycerined foliage, leafless branches and silk flowers can be inserted directly in the potting compost.

❖

OUTER CONTAINERS

To protect the furniture it rests on, the outer container should be waterproof. As long as it is well lined with flexible plastic attached with sellotape or fitted with a waterproof inner container, almost anything, even glamorous cardboard gift boxes, can be used.

All sorts of baskets – and even upturned straw hats – make excellent containers, and hoop-like handles can support climbing house plants or cut foliage such as ivy or creeping fig. In the case of a loose or open-weave container, line it with sphagnum moss first, then use an inner lining of plastic. Keep the moss fresh by mist-spraying regularly.

As well as baskets, you can use any sort of kitchen container – mixing bowls, wooden fruit boxes from greengrocers, woks on stands or bamboo steaming baskets. A wide-necked jug can contain a small house plant as well as cut material. For a formal, dining-table centrepiece, use tureens or serving bowls.

Footed or stemmed containers such as large brandy snifters or raised punch bowls are ideal for pot et fleurs that contain arching or trailing material. You can also create vertical space by placing the container on a stool or small table.

From the garden or garden centre, there are wooden trugs, galvanised metal buckets and wide, shallow terracotta pots. Seasonal containers can be made from hollowed-out fruits or vegetables, and moss or fresh waxy leaves can be glued onto plastic food storage containers in overlapping rows.

For larger containers, use fish tanks or old glass battery tanks lined with moss; log baskets; umbrella holders; wooden toy chests and old wooden cradles and Moses baskets.

For wall-hung pot et fleurs, you can use terracotta half pots, designed specifically for the purpose, or wire pot holders, screwed to the wall. Alternatively, hang up rigid wicker or wire bicycle baskets or even traditional wicker fishermen's bags.

LEFT A selection of containers suitable for pot et fleurs: jugs, trugs, baskets, china bowls and galvanised metal buckets... you can use anything that comes to hand.

HOUSE PLANTS AND CONTAINERS

The house plants can either remain in their pots and the space between them be filled with florist's foam or potting compost, or be removed from their pots and planted directly into nutrient-rich loam-based potting compost. Leaving house plants in their pots makes it easier to remove and replace a plant that fails, and to vary watering and feeding regimens, if necessary.

If you remove the pot, flatten the rootballs of the plant a little by rolling them between your hands, or squeeze them together to fit in the container. The containers should be deep enough to allow the surface of the rootball of the largest house plant to come 2.5–4cm (1–1½in) below the rim, for ease of watering. Given good potting compost and regular feeding in the growing season, the plants should thrive. For containers much deeper than the pots or rootballs, invert a flowerpot or use tightly crumpled wire mesh to serve as a base.

❖

COMPOSITE CONTAINERS

Instead of a single large container, individual containers can be clustered together and filled with house plants, cut flowers or both. Cups and saucers or drinking mugs are ideal for miniature pot et fleurs; on a larger scale, display a row or cluster of white china vases, some filled with plants, others with cut flowers.

You can use one container on top of another, the larger, broader one serving as a base: perhaps a plain cake stand or old-fashioned ham-carving stand, with a smaller, more vertical container on top, stabilised with a bit of household mastic, if necessary. Collections of stoneware, Parian or blue and white jugs, copper or ceramic jelly moulds, Wedgwood containers, teapots or tea caddies are excellent sources for multiple pot et fleur displays, as are items in a range of sizes such as soufflé dishes with different diameters.

'Composite' can also refer to the container itself: a container can have a flat base such as a breadboard or cheeseboard, and sides made of a ring of florist's foam packed with flowers or foliage.

THE RAW MATERIAL

❖ ❖ ❖

ealthy house plants, and cut flowers or foliage are best bought from a reputable source with a rapid turnover such as high-street chain shops, garden departments of major DIY centres or supermarket chains. Ideally they should be in fat bud with one or two blooms open to ensure both sufficient maturity and maximum display life.

❖

BUYING HOUSE PLANTS AND CUT FLOWERS

Plants should be healthy looking, compact with short joints and good leaf colour for the type, well balanced and symmetrical (apart from bonsai and some irregular- shaped plants such as Christmas cactus and *Aeonium arboreum*). Foliage should extend to the base except where plants are naturally bare-stemmed, such as the Madagascar dragon tree. Avoid plants with wilted, unnaturally pale or yellow leaves, or brown leaf tips and margins. One or two leaves from a small plant can be safely picked off but removing disfigured leaves from a rubber plant or aspidistra may leave permanent gaps.

When buying a new plant always check the flower buds, the growing tips of the stems and the leaves, especially the undersides, for signs of pests and diseases. Check the base, or crown, of plants such as cyclamen and African violet, which are vulnerable to rotting crowns and avoid any with slimy leaves or dark, slimy stem bases. Be wary of plants in slimy pots or with roots growing out of the base, unless like clivia and hippeastrum the plant prefers pot-bound conditions. Rootballs loosely held in the pot are also suspect. When transporting the plant ensure it has a polythene sleeve to protect it against draughts – in cold weather it should be insulated against cold in a carrier bag or a box; in hot weather remember not to leave it in a parked car.

For pot et fleurs that need to make an immediate impact flowering plants in full bloom are showier and may also be cheaper as their display life is shorter. Cut flowers in full bloom need checking for signs of ageing – drooping blooms or browning of petals are obvious, but other specific signs are: lower florets missing from spiky plants such as delphiniums, cymbidiums and freesias; empty calyces on spray carnations; fluffy yellow rather than hard, tightly packed centres on daisy-like flowers such as single chrysanthemums and Michelmas daisies; papery translucence at the edges of thin-petalled flowers such as iris and daffodils.

The length of time in bloom varies greatly from flower to flower. Some flowers, such as amaryllis, anthurium, banksia, bird-of-paradise, carnations and spray carnations, china asters, chincherinchees, chrysanthemums, cymbidiums, echinops, gerberas, ginger lilies, mature hydrangea heads, proteas, sea holly and statice, can go on literally for weeks. Others, such as ceanothus, clematis, hellebores, mimosa, poppies, sweet peas, violets and zinnias, no matter how well they are conditioned and maintained, are fleeting pleasures.

❖

FOLIAGE, MOSS AND LICHEN

Some foliage such as box, butcher's broom, camellia, eucalyptus, ivy and skimmia are naturally long-lasting when cut, while others such as many ferns are not. Choose cut foliage with healthy-looking, turgid leaves, and avoid any with slimy or rotting stems. Yellowing fronds on asparagus ferns are signs of old age. Shiny-leaved evergreens such as box, euonymus and holly take on a dull appearance if they've been out of water for a long time; cut eucalyptus foliage becomes stiff and inflexible with age.

Given the cost and lack of commercially available foliage it is best if at all possible to grow your own. Most useful are small to medium-sized, broad-leaved evergreens in plain and variegated forms: elaeagnus, camellia, euonymus, garrya, Portugal laurel, small-leaved cherry laurels, box, cotoneaster, Mexican orange myrtle, skimmia and viburnum. Plain and variegated-leaved ivies can be

LEFT A reliable local garden centre and florist are undoubtedly important, but a quick scout around your own kitchen, garden or potting shed can often yield unexpected treasures for pot et fleurs.

the smallest space while only the larger garden will have room for the large-leaved evergreens such as ordinary laurel, evergreen magnolia and rhododendron.

Using moss or lichen is the easiest way of concealing the pot and potting compost in a pot et fleur. Both sphagnum moss and the less widely available bun moss will keep fresh for several weeks, refridgerated in a polythene bag. Alternatively, you can plant clumps of selaginella or baby's tears directly into the peat or potting compost of a pot et fleur.

$\mathscr{P}$RACTICALITIES

❖ ❖ ❖

$\mathscr{M}$ost of the practical side of pot et fleur is common sense, keeping in mind that you are dealing, at least in part, with living things. Clean, sharp tools; clean equipment and containers, well conditioned cut material and well cared-for house plants, with a steady supply of water and nutrients according to type and season, result in a display that remains attractive for the longest possible time.

❖

BASIC CONDITIONING OF FLOWERS AND FOLIAGE

Whenever a stem is cut, an air block forms at the base, hindering or preventing further uptake of water; generally, the longer a cut stem is out of water, the less it can conduct water to reach the foliage or blooms. Immediately before inserting them in water or saturated florist's foam, always re-cut the stems of cut flowers and foliage, slightly above the previous cut and at an angle, to expose the maximum surface area to the water. This can extend their display life for up to two weeks. Ideally, cut the stem end under water to prevent any possibility of an air block. If you are cutting material from your garden, it is best to carry a bucket part-filled with water and put the material into it straight away.

❖

Variations

Stems from plants such as euphorbia and poppy which are filled with milky sap are treated differently. To stop the flow of sap, dip the cut ends in boiling water, or sear with a match. The white portions of the stems of tulips and other bulb flowers cannot take up water and should be removed. Hollow stems such as delphiniums and dahlias should be upended, filled with water and plugged with cotton wool, then placed in water immediately.

Crushing the lowest 5cm (2in) of woody stems such as roses, chrysanthemums, lilacs and chaenomeles was once recommended. Now, just scraping off the bottom 5cm (2in) of bark, where practical, is considered less likely to encourage rot; it is also easier to insert scraped, rather than crushed, stems into florist's foam.

❖

Final Preparations

Strip off any leaves that would be under water, to prevent rotting; the dull-looking leaves of dahlias, alstroemerias, lilacs, chrysanthemums and philadelphus should also be discarded as they often wilt or turn yellow long before the flowers die, besides competing with them for water. If you wish, use a disposable razor to strip the thorns from roses to make them easier to handle.

Cut off the tiny, uppermost buds of gladioli, tuberoses and kaffir lilies, since they won't open anyway, and detract from the general appearance of the flower spike. Use manicure scissors to cut the stamens from the centre of lilies before arranging, since the fiercely yellow or orange pollen stains both the petals and any fabric with which it comes into contact.

If possible, stand the conditioned flowers or foliage in a deep container of tepid water for several hours or overnight, so that they are fully turgid. Hostas and thin-leaved foliage such as ferns benefit from being completely submerged in tepid water overnight, as does slightly immature foliage such as beech in late spring and early summer. Mature foliage is usually longer lasting than young foliage.

❖

Basic Cut Flower and Foliage Care

A few drops of bleach added to cut flower water helps prevent bacteria forming, which stops the water smelling and the stems rotting. Bleach also removes the un-floral smell of members of the cabbage family, such as stocks, and of the onion family, such as ornamental onions. Alternatively, use cut-flower food, which contains an anti-bacterial agent, following the instructions on the packet.

Most cut flowers last longer in cool, draught-free conditions and dislike exposure to direct sunlight, heat, gas fumes and sudden temperature changes. If you use cut flower food, always top up containers or florist's foam with fresh water as necessary – flowers drink more water than you'd expect, especially in warm conditions. If you use bleach, change the water regularly and, if practical, scrub out the container and re-cut the stems at the same time.

Re-cut the stems every few days, especially if they start to change colour or become soft – chrysanthemums, in particular. Some flowers are longer-lasting than others; check the display daily and remove wilted flowers which may spoil the rest of the display (decaying flowers and foliage give off gas fumes which can shorten the life of some other flowers, such as freesias and iris). Long-lasting flowers such as gerberas or chincherinchees will serve as an ongoing framework while shorter-lived flowers are replaced with fresh blooms. If soft-stemmed flowers start to wilt prematurely, re-cutting the stem end and plunging to the neck in hand-hot water often helps. With soft-stemmed foliage, do the same, but submerge the foliage completely. With woody-stemmed flowers and foliage, try re-cutting, dipping the stem end in boiling water for a few seconds, then soaking in hand-hot water. Some flower arrangers swear by submerging wilted roses in tepid water for several hours to revive them.

❖

Basic House Plant Care

The more similar the needs of the different plants in a pot et fleur, particlarly a long-term display, the easier it is to meet them. In general, house plants dislike draughty conditions near ill-fitting doors or windows or in the direct line of air conditioners, and exposure to a direct source of heat or to gas or coal fumes is also damaging.

❖

Heat and Light

Though a few popular house plants, including stephanotis, African violet, anthurium, angels' wings and gardenia need a minimum of 16 C (60 F), more house plants die from heat than from cold in today's centrally heated homes. If in doubt, keep it cool. House plants 'borrowed' from temperate climate gardens such as forced hyacinths, daffodils, hydrangeas, ivy, lilies, polyanthus and miniature roses definitely like cool bright conditions, as do the slightly tender 'near misses' such as cyclamen, indoor jasmine, passionflower and azaleas.

In late autumn and winter, move plants closer to windows to provide enough sunlight. In late spring and summer, most plants must be protected from solar gain, and moved away from south- or west-facing windows. As a general rule, the thinner the leaf, the more protection it needs from direct sunlight and the more it appreciates humidity. Variegated plants such as coleus and crotons need bright light for the most intense colour, although thin-leafed variegated plants grow best in light shade. Most flowering plants need good light to form buds but plants bought with fat buds showing colour will flower given just a little light.

❖

Food and Water

Most house plants are sold in peat-based potting compost, which contains about a month's supply of nutrients, after which you have to supply your own – concentrated liquid, powder, granules or slow-release fertiliser tablets. There are also quick-acting foliar feeds, fertilisers specifically for foliage plants, or for flowering plants, and specialist fertilisers for orchids, citrus trees, African violets, cacti and succulents.

Most house plants in active growth and/or flower need weekly or fortnightly feeding in addition to regular watering, although too much feeding causes weak, straggly growth that is vulnerable to pests and diseases. In late autumn and winter, water resting house plants every week or two, just enough to prevent potting compost drying out completely. Over-watering is far more liable to be fatal than under-watering; sun-loving plants such as desert cacti and succulents are especially vulnerable. Remember that pot et fleur containers generally lack drainage holes, so check that no water is sitting in the bottom. A few plants, however, such as the umbrella house plant, like saturated potting compost all year round. With house plants that are liable to rot if water rests on the leaves, crowns or tubers, such as cyclamen and African violets, water from beneath if possible.

❖

BASIC TOOLS AND EQUIPMENT

You can buy most, if not all, of the tools and equipment you need at a garden centre; your florist should be able to supply information on specialist florists' sundries.

SECATEURS, ideally with precision ground stainless steel blades, are needed for cutting tough or woody stems, such as roses or chrysanthemums. Scissor-action, or parrot's-beak secateurs, with a double cutting edge, are less liable to crush stems than anvil-type secateurs that have one cutting and one flat edge.

SCISSORS are useful for cutting through softer stems, raffia and ribbons; florist's scissors, though expensive, are long lasting and can cut through wire. There are several sizes, weights and types, with round or blunt ends; try them out in your hand before choosing. Manicure scissors are helpful for fiddly work – removing stamens from lilies, for example.

KNIVES, ideally stainless steel and with a selection of blade lengths, are useful for scraping stems and cutting and shaping florist's foam.

FLORIST'S FOAM comes mainly in rectangular blocks, but special shapes such as rings, cylinders, globes and cones are also available. Fresh-flower florist's foam is usually green, of quite a dense, soft, crumbly consistency and must be saturated before use. (Let the foam blocks float in a deep sink full of water – don't hold them down or under the tap). Dried-flower florist's foam is grey and has a more open, harder texture; neither can be substituted for the other. You can also buy inexpensive plastic bases to fit rectangular and cylindrical foam blocks; foam rings come with plastic bases attached.

FLORIST'S SPIKES AND MASTIC Sometimes called florist's frogs, these plastic spikes are attached to the base of a container with a blob of florist's mastic, and a block of florist's foam is impaled on the spike. Florist's oil-based mastic, sometimes called adhesive clay, is usually green and sold on a reel; blue household mastic is equally suitable. Fresh florist's foam generally keeps its position when saturated, especially if it is wedged into an outer container; spikes are more useful with dried-flower florist's foam.

WIRE MESH NETTING, or chicken wire, is useful for large scale displays which would be too heavy for florist's foam; and it can also be wrapped round one or more blocks of florist's foam, to reinforce it. Some cut material, such as daffodils, smoke bush and most silver and grey foliage, cannot absorb water from florist's foam, so it is better to use wire-mesh netting.

Buy 15–50mm (½–2in) galvanised mesh, according to the size of the container and stems to be inserted – remember that it can be difficult to insert stems into small-hole wire mesh once it is crumpled.

WIRE CUTTERS are useful for cutting wire-mesh netting regularly; never use ordinary kitchen scissors or secateurs to cut netting, as it ruins the blades.

MIST SPRAYERS increase the humidity around house plants and flowers; buy inexpensive plastic models or use thoroughly cleaned-out window-sprayers.

DUST SHEETS are useful if your workspace also doubles as a dining room, or is carpeted. You can cut up big plastic dustbin-liners to protect floors and work surfaces – they are also ideal for lining non-waterproof baskets or other containers.

NARROW, LONG-SPOUTED WATERING CANS are easier to manoeuvre than ordinary, garden-scale watering cans – this is important when pot et fleur displays are on polished wood or other vulnerable surfaces, or anywhere near electronic equipment!

GARDEN TROWELS are useful for handling potting compost.

CROCKS can provide a drainage layer in the base of outer containers, as well as elevating flower pots in very deep cache pots. Use broken pieces of terracotta, pebbles or gravel.

$\mathcal{S}$PRING

❖ ❖ ❖

$\mathcal{T}$HE RAW MATERIAL FOR SPRING POT ET FLEURS IS SO LUSH AND SEDUC-
TIVE, ESPECIALLY AFTER WINTER'S PAUCITY, THAT IT IS ALMOST IMPOSSIBLE
TO GO WRONG. $\mathcal{I}$F THERE IS A PLANT, CUT FLOWER OR FOLIAGE THAT YOU
ESPECIALLY LIKE, USE IT AS THE KEYSTONE OF A DISPLAY, AND THEN YOU
CAN BE AS IMAGINATIVE OR INNOVATIVE AS YOU LIKE IN YOUR CHOICE OF
ADDITIONAL MATERIAL.

❖ ❖ ❖

As well as the natural, seasonal influx of garden and florists' flowers, spring offers a wealth of raw material from less obvious sources. Mundane seasonal garden chores, for example, can provide masses of pot et fleur ingredients. 'Rubbish' from pruning shrubs that flower on new growth, clipping evergreen hedges, removing suckers from the base of grafted plants can, instead of being consigned to the bonfire, be used in pot et fleur displays, and add a personal touch to store-bought mixed baskets. Even moss scraped from shady paths, gutters and paving can provide a 'moss garden' finished surface to the pot et fleur.

Small, spring-flowering garden bulbs, biennials and perennials, dug up with a generous rootball, are ideal for short-term pot et fleurs. Try to display them in a cool spot and provide cool nights, returning them to the garden afterwards to make a full recovery. The stems of many small, spring-flowering bulbs are too delicate to insert into florist's foam, as are the stems of biennials such as bellis, pansy and polyanthus, so displaying them with roots intact solves a technical problem. Alternatively, use them as cut flowers inserted in a concealed container of water.

A forage through an early spring garden may yield many different plants in flower, but only one or two blossoms of each – lungwort, perhaps, primroses, grape hyacinths, leopard's bane, periwinkle and the last of the Algerian iris. For instant elegance, display them in a forest of water-filled wine glasses, one glass per type, interspersed with moss-filled wine glasses, around a large, central house plant or group of house plants.

In high spring, cut ribbon-like lengths of *Clematis montana* in bloom, and wind them round the base of a wide, mixed planting dish, or encircle a cluster of small house plants and flower-filled vases on a long, dining room table, or garland the stem and branches of a weeping fig, much as a clematis grows in nature. You can also spiral clematis round the sides of a tall, slim, pot et fleur container or the handle of a plant-filled basket.

For large-scale impact, use the long branches of spring-flowering

LEFT For a reliable green and white infill, suitable for almost any pot et fleur, raid the garden for Mexican orange blossom, with its sharply aromatic leaves. Alternatively, use gypsophila from the florist, filled out with cut green foliage such as laurustinus or even privet.

Plants
BUSY LIZZIE
CAPE PRIMROSE
DUMB CANE

Cut Flowers and Foliage
4–6 BRANCHES OF MEXICAN ORANGE

1 Place the dumb cane, off centre, at the back of a basket or other deep container.
2 Place the Cape primrose and busy Lizzie towards the front, evenly spaced, so that, with the dumb cane, they form a triangle.
3 Pack the spaces between with saturated florist's foam, wedged tightly to fit.
4 Insert the Mexican orange branches in the florist's foam, hiding the foam block and filling the gaps between the house plants and breaking the harsh line of the basket rim. Check from all angles as you proceed.

25

RIGHT Nothing could be further apart, in horticultural terms, than the hardy biennial forget-me-not and tender, tropical African violets. Yet they look stunning together, partnered here with lungwort, another hardy garden plant. Condition lungwort foliage by submerging it for several hours or overnight in cool water. The rustic wooden basket is painted toning purple, but can be whitewashed and repainted to match other floral colour schemes.

Plants
2 AFRICAN VIOLETS

Cut Flowers and Foliage
1 LARGE BUNCH OF FORGET-ME-NOTS
8-10 LUNGWORT LEAVES

1 Position 2 African violet plants, diagonally opposite, in a rectangular wooden basket or other container.
2 Place water-filled jars in the opposite corners of the container, then insert bunches of forget-me-nots in each jar.
3 Use lungwort leaves to form a ruffle around the forget-me-nots. Position the leaves to conceal the jars and arch over the edge of the basket.

shrubs such as flowering currant, forsythia, philadelphus, spiraea, mahonia, Mexican orange and kerria to add height and bright colour to foliage house plants.

❖

CUT FLOWERING BRANCHES
Flowering cherry and other ornamental members of the *Rosaceae* family such as flowering plums, peaches and crab-apples, symbolise spring. Cut a single branch, ideally with natural curves, in fat bud and impale it on a pin holder set in either a container of water, a mossy dish or basket, or one with a permanent 'ground cover' of club moss, mind-your-own-business, or baby's tears. Arrange the branch so that it arches, semi-horizontally, over clumps of growing primulas, scillas or grape hyacinths. Try to use a long, relatively shallow container – rectangular Japanese moribana containers with solid glazed sides are ideal – to repeat the lines of the fruit blossom. If wished, use an interestingly shaped rock or piece of driftwood at the base of the branch, to suggest a landscape.

Fruit blossom is delicate and generally short lived, but you can replace the cut branch every few days as necessary and, provided you keep the plants well fed – water-soluble foliar feeding is a good idea for primulas – and watered, the display can go on for two or more weeks. To ring the changes, replace the spent blossom with branches from different flowering trees, including 'proper' fruit trees. For extra colour from foliage, there are purple-leafed varieties of cherry plum, *Prunus cerasifera* 'Atropurpurea', and *P.c.* 'Nigra' – ideal with the rich purple leaves of rex begonia varieties or the eyelash begonia.

Camellias and magnolias are the two most dramatic shrubs to flower in early-to-mid spring, and single, well chosen branches of either can be inserted into the clump-forming house plants such as white sails or peace lilies or into a dense, sprawling peppermint geranium with its large, velvety grey leaves.

Both camellia and magnolia are slow growing, however, and if you can take only a small sprig with one or two buds, try inserting it

ABOVE AND LEFT Kalenchoes and
pansies alternating in a simple
earthenware bowl form the basis
for the two different displays
shown, but there are plenty of
other variations.

Plants
3 KALENCHOES
2 PANSIES

Cut Flowers and Foliage
3–4 STEMS OF *KERRIA JAPONICA*
1 BUNCH OF SOLIDASTER

1 *Alternate the pansies and
kalenchoes in a deep round bowl,
and pack the centre and space
between the pots with saturated
florist's foam.*
2 *Insert tall stems of kerria and
solidaster in the middle, to create
a fountain-like effect, and
shorter stems round the edge, to
create a ruffle.*

horizontally, Oriental fashion, into the potting compost of a low-growing, wide-spreading foliage plant such as silver net leaf, prayer plant or creeping fig. Or combine a sprig of camellia on a mounded mossy 'knoll' with a potted fern such as the button fern and some curvaceous, arching overhead stems of pussy willow.

You can buy a small camellia shrub in flower – some have stems that seem almost too slender to support their heavy blooms – to use in a pot et fleur, before planting it in the garden.

RIGHT This display, with its
lemons, is ideal for Shrove
Tuesday; if you don't have bay,
use laurustinus or Portugal
laurel instead.

Plants
3 KALENCHOES
2 PANSIES

*Cut Flowers and
Foliage*
1 BUNCH OF SINGAPORE ORCHIDS
1 BRANCH OF BAY
LEMONS

*1 Alternate the pansies and
kalenchoes in a deep round bowl,
and pack the centre and any
space between the pots with
saturated florist's foam.
2 Insert the Singapore orchids in
the middle and gently tuck
sprigs of bay leaves and lemons
between the kalenchoes and
pansies.*

Chaenomeles, or flowering or Japanese quince, is a reliable, cottage-garden toughie. Small, flower-studded branches from it can enhance a big specimen of variegated piggyback plant or large branches can be arranged to 'grow' from the base of a grape ivy.

Towards the end of spring, azaleas and rhododendrons come into their own. Use the elegantly-shaped branches of azalea in blossom instead of cut fruit blossom to form the tree-like canopy above a clump

RIGHT This compact, all-white arrangement combines the formality of a triangular outline with the lushness of lilacs in full bloom. Equally suitable for weddings or dinner parties, the display contains a small variegated weeping fig, surprisingly inexpensive and worth its weight in gold, for year-round pot et fleur work. Try to choose a spreading, multi-stemmed specimen.

Plants
VARIEGATED WEEPING FIG

Cut Flowers and Foliage
12 STEMS OF LILAC, STRIPPED OF LEAVES
2 STEMS OF IRIS

1 Place the weeping fig off centre and towards the back in a deep oval or rectangular container.
2 Pack the spaces between with saturated florist's foam, wedged tightly to fit.
3 Insert the lilac into the foam block either side and in front of the weeping fig, to form a triangular outline. Angle some to arch over the rim of the container.
4 Lastly, insert the 2 irises, one cut slightly shorter than the other, in the centre.

of small, flowering garden plants or house plants. The heavy globe-like flower heads of rhododendron need equally substantial house plant partners such as the huge-leafed tree philodendron or lacy tree philodendron.

Lilacs add fragrance as well as old-fashioned beauty but their leaves are best removed, for while they add nothing to the display, they rob the blooms of water, causing them to wilt prematurely. Cut the stripped stems to varying lengths and insert them in amongst either the loose, arrow-shaped leaves of a goosefoot plant, the needle-like foliage of a Buddhist pine or the vertical foliage of mother-in-law's tongue.

Use the linear branches of flowering broom to create an explosive effect in a pot et fleur, radiating them outwards, upwards and downwards from an imaginary central point; or arrange just a few, tightly packed sprays to arch from one side like a rooster's tail, or vertically like an exclamation mark.

❖

CATKINS
Leafless branches in catkin, such as hazel, alder, hornbeam and pussy willow, are an early spring feature. Insert branches into potting compost or packed florist's foam in a container of mixed, low-growing house plants such as ivy, fittonias, variegated miniature sweet flag or azaleas. Leafless contorted hazel adds Eastern impact to the already Oriental elegance of aspidistra, perhaps with cut rhododendron blossom in the foreground, to complete the vignette. Cut willow branches may break into leaf and even root in moist potting compost, and you can plant them out when you dismantle the display.

❖

CUT SPRING FOLIAGE IDEAS
Young spring foliage can be too thin to last well when cut but mature evergreen foliage and, later in spring, new growth can be used. The shiny-leafed, upright suckers of *Rhododendron ponticum* that grow at the bases of grafted varieties should be removed in spring, to prevent them overwhelming the named variety. These suckers are

excellent in a large-scale pot et fleur, perhaps adding substance to a leggy cane begonia such as the angel's wing begonia, the spotted angel's wing begonia, or to an out-of-flower abutilon, with a focal point of cut flowers. The upright branches could form the vertical backdrop to a front-facing, shallow 'woodland' dish garden display of cut hellebores and potted ferns embedded in moss. Removing all-green shoots from variegated shrubs such as myrtle and privet is equally rewarding; their multi-branched growth habit makes them excellent for inserting in baskets of mixed house plants.

Use spring clippings from small-leafed evergreen hedges, such as box or evergreen honeysuckle, to make a 'hedge' around a shallow, miniature dish garden filled with primroses, cowslips, auriculas, tiny violas or grape hyacinths embedded in moss. Insert the clippings directly into potting compost – they may well root – or into saturated florist's foam. For larger versions, use Portugal laurel clippings; laurel itself is too big for pot et fleur 'hedging'.

Cutting back pelargoniums is another spring-time task which has a hidden benefit, for the prunings of scented-leafed species and varieties are especially lovely inserted in pot et fleurs. If inserted in damp, peat-based potting compost, the prunings will usually root and can be potted up separately.

Leaves from early hostas are fantastic value in pot et fleurs, and they are less liable to be damaged by slugs than later in the season.

❖

SPRING PERENNIALS

Violets are as modest in their display as camellias and magnolias are showy. Completely submerge freshly cut or bought violets in a glass of water for a few minutes, maximising their water content, then place them in bunches in tiny, water-filled phials or jars sunk in the potting compost of a shallow container already filled with thin-leafed ferns such as maidenhair and bird's-nest fern. Cover the potting compost with moss and place a bell jar or glass cake or cheese cover over the entire display. This keeps the display humid and also concentrates the fragrance so that, when you lift the lid, a waft of concentrated

RIGHT Pot et fleur encompasses cut flowers and house plants displayed next to each other, as well as those in a single container. Containers that are similar in material, such as this enamelled metal bucket and jug, help to reinforce the sense of unity. The stocks are members of the cabbage family, but a few drops of bleach in the vase water will prevent them smelling of cabbage.

Plants
VARIEGATED IVY

Cut Flowers and Foliage
2 BUNCHES OF *EUSTOMA GRANDIFLORUM*
2 BUNCHES OF BROMPTON STOCKS

1 Place a variegated ivy in a bucket, raising it on bricks or crumpled mesh netting if necessary.
2 Loosely combine the eustoma and stocks, and insert them in a water-filled jug or similar container.

scent is released. Alternatively, you can dig up and plant violets in moss-covered potting compost, to create a tapestry-like foundation for a pot et fleur.

The tight, dense roots of primulas, polyanthus and auriculas are ideal for planting in pot et fleurs. Plant one, two or three in a bed of moss or baby's tears, together with a small umbrella plant and a

LEFT AND RIGHT Variegated ivy,
crotons and begonias are common
enough, and perhaps even a little
boring-looking as individual
house plants, but their different
shapes make an impact when put
together as the basis for a pot et
fleur.

Plants
CROTON
2 VARIEGATED IVIES
TUBEROUS-ROOTED BEGONIA

*Cut Flowers and
Foliage*
1 BUNCH OF DOUBLE TULIPS
3 BRANCHES OF GOLDEN-LEAFED
MEXICAN ORANGE.

*1 Place the croton at the back of
a deep basket, then place an ivy
on each side in the front and the
begonia in the middle.
2 Pack the spaces between the
pots and the basket with
saturated florist's foam.
3 Insert the double tulips in the
front and sides to fill the space
between the ivies, then add
sprigs of Mexican orange to
build up density in the centre.*

curved willow branch. Auricula flowers are exquisitely sophisticated,
and often very subtly coloured, compared with the brashness of most
polyanthus. A cut and tightly packed bunch of auricula blooms would
be lovely with the velvety leaves of purple passion vine or with bronze-
coloured pileas. You can also copy the Victorians and pot up
good-sized perennials such as Solomon's seal, bleeding heart and, in
early spring, hostas, for short-term pot et fleurs in a cool room.

Lily-of-the-valley is sometimes listed under perennials in gardening
books and catalogues, other times under bulbs, rhizomes and tubers.
Stems placed vertically in a bed of growing club moss can make a

lovely miniature 'forest', perhaps interspersed with sprigs of rue.

Hellebores are notoriously difficult to condition but rewardingly exquisite as cut blooms; plunge them in deep pails of water, slit the bottom 5cm (2in) of stalk and arrange them with strongly arching cut material such as berberis, or dense, clump-forming house plants such as queen's tears or painted drop-tongue, as they will help to support the nodding heads.

The green flowers of *Helleborus foetidus* and *H. lividus corsicus* are ideal for all-green pot et fleur displays; and the pinky-purply-dusky range of Lenten roses suits purple-tinged foliage such as cut stems of *Mahonia japonica* and the purple-leafed form of the succulent house plant *Aeonium arboreum* 'Atropurpureum' or various bronze-leafed pileas.

Peonies and flag iris are sumptuous, late-spring treats and their sturdy stems make them easy to use in pot et fleurs with florist's foam foundations. Combine them with equally bold house plants: pink, rose or white peonies with variegated caladiums, or iris with grassy-leafed house plants such as variegated Japanese sedge or variegated white lily turf.

❖

Spring Biennials

Wallflowers – actually perennials, though usually discarded after flowering – can be dug up when just about to flower and brought indoors to bloom; they have surprisingly tiny root systems and several can be planted in quite a small basket. Their woody stems make wallflowers trickier as cut blooms, and they last longest when cut fairly short, 7.5-10cm (3-4in), and given several hours' soak in warm water before being arranged. If you grow mixed wallflowers, cut a sprig or two from different coloured flowers and insert them, tightly bunched, among the fronds of a maidenhair fern.

Forget-me-nots, genuine biennials that die after setting seed, are very long lasting when cut and, if you have them in your garden, chances are you have them on a large scale, since they self seed easily. Use them generously, almost like gypsophila, to add lightness to

LEFT If you have a laburnum, or a friendly neighbour with a laburnum, this couldn't be easier! Laburnum flowers, like lilac, last longer when stripped of foliage. To condition them, scrape the bark off the lowest 5cm (2in), then leave in warm water for several hours or overnight.

Plants
CROTON
2 VARIEGATED IVIES
TUBEROUS-ROOTED BEGONIA

Cut Flowers and Foliage
5-6 LABURNUM FLOWER CLUSTERS

1 Place the croton at the back of a deep basket, then place an ivy on each side in the front and the begonia in the middle.
2 Pack the spaces between the pots and the basket with saturated florist's foam.
3 Insert the laburnum flower clusters in the spaces between the ivies so that the golden flowers trail over the rim of the basket and hide the foam.

RIGHT A garden trug gives a pot
et fleur a 'just-picked' freshness,
however exotic the actual raw
material is, and by resting the
display on a chair, as here, you
can perpetuate the gentle
illusion.

Plants
VARIEGATED IVY

*Cut Flowers and
Foliage*
2 BRANCHES OF MAHONIA IN
BERRY
1 BUNCH OF LIATRIS

*1 Place some saturated florist's
foam in the middle of a lined
trug. Place the ivy in front, in
one corner.*
*2 Insert a mahonia branch in
each end of the foam, behind the
ivy. Then insert the liatris stems
individually, but tightly, to give
the effect of a bunch.*

a bought basket of mixed house plants, or as a floral collar round
another bunch of flowers – rosebuds for example – in a pot et fleur.

The old-fashioned and diminutive double daisy is another vague-
ly perennial or biennial plant. Plant it under the spreading, oak-like
bows of a large jade plant, perhaps with a box twig 'hedge' or an
outer circle of small-leafed ivy.

Garden centres sell reasonably priced trays of biennials such as
polyanthus, pansies and delicate violas in flower. Before a dinner
party or other social occasion, buy a tray of them and plant up an
attractive basket or pottery container, using moss as 'ground cover'
and perhaps an edging or a more intricate, parterre-like arrangement of box twigs. After the event, but in any case before they show
signs of flagging, plant them out.

❖

FLOWERING BULBS

Hardy flowering bulbs can be dug up from the garden, or bought
in bud or flower from garden centres, enjoyed as part of a pot et fleur
for a short time indoors, then planted outdoors or discarded. You
always pay substantially more for containerised bulbs sold in bloom
than dormant bulbs you plant or pot up and grow yourself, but containerised bulbs in bloom are convenient for last-minute displays,
and if you plant them out afterwards, they pay for themselves
many times over in future years.

Daffodils have strongly directional blooms and arranging the larger hybrids in mixed, cut flower displays can be awkward, but pots
of miniature narcissi, sold in bloom at garden centres, fit easily into
pot et fleurs, perhaps combined with pots of pale blue *Anemone blan-
da* or the slightly sinister snake's-head fritillary in flower. Garden
centres also sell pots of charming dwarf tulips in flower, such as the
variegated-leafed *Tulipa* 'Red Riding Hood'.

Forced hyacinths are available in deepest winter but hyacinths are
really spring garden plants. They are often sold in single pots; buy
several and display them intertwined with long, trailing sprays of
ivy or, if you're lucky enough to have it, the pale greeny yellow blooms

RIGHT Pink and green variegated angel wings, variegated green and white dumb cane foliage and pink gerbera flowers are mutually enhancing. Gerberas are relatively expensive but last a long time.

Plants
ANGEL WINGS
DUMB CANE

Cut Flowers and Foliage
5 GERBERAS

1 Place the dumb cane towards the back of a round bowl, and the angel wings in the front.
2 Pack the space between them with saturated florist's foam.
3 Cut the gerberas to varying heights and insert in the foam.

of the evergreen, fern-leafed clematis, *Clematis cirrhosa balearica* – hyacinths are generally over by the time *Clematis montana* blooms.

If you prepare your own bulbs for forcing and have an ongoing display over several weeks or even months, there is often an over-lap when earlier forced bulbs have grown lank arching stems but the flowers are still worth displaying; cut them and intersperse them amongst pots filled with erect-stemmed, growing hyacinths.

Tuberous-rooted Turk's cap ranunculus comes in a range of intense and subtle colours, with a growth habit – large, blowsy flowers on straight, leafless stems, with a basal rosette of tiny leaves – reminiscent of a child's drawing of a flower. They are sold as inexpensive house or greenhouse plants and as cut flowers. For a spectacular centrepiece, plant a formal 'field' of one colour of ranunculus in a large dish, covering the surface with moss, or display cut ranunculus, their ends inserted individually in orchid phials, nestling among Boston fern or asparagus fern.

Crown imperials in bold oranges and yellows are sold in flower and a trio rising above pussy willow stems would look magnificent.

You can pleasantly muddle the seasons – much as the seventeenth-century Dutch flower painters did – by combining miniature rose house plants, available all year round, with quintessentially spring bulb blooms such as cut grape hyacinths or scillas, or even with winter snowdrops in a mossy container, with ivy in mini-pots or sprigs of cut ivy as 'ground cover'. Alternatively, muddle your plant geography: combine handsome, unfurling horse chestnut branches with miniature narcissi in concealed pots and the star-like rosettes of miniature earth stars, natives of Brazil, set in moss.

❖

ALPINES FOR MINIATURE POT ET FLEURS

Alpines are outdoor plants, needing plenty of ventilation and cool conditions, but they, too, can do temporary duty indoors. Spring marks the start of plant sales for horticultural societies and charities where big clumps of aubrieta, arabis, alyssum, London pride and mossy saxifrages can often be found in flower. You can also lift and divide mature clumps in gardens, even when they are in bud or flower, although it is usually done after flowering. Place the flowering clumps in shallow baskets filled with potting compost and insert a few stems of greeny-black snake's-head or mourning iris.

Garden centres sell spring-flowering alpine plants in containers

BELOW AND RIGHT Here hostas and pansies form the basis of two different, but equally easy, pot et fleurs.

Plants
HOSTA SIEBOLDIANA
1-3 PANSIES

Cut Flowers and Foliage
1 BUNCH OF *EUPHORBIA ROBBIAE*
1 BUNCH OF TULIPS
1 BUNCH OF ANEMONES

1 Place the hosta, in its pot, towards the back of a trug and the pansy or pansies, in their pots, in front. If they have been dug up from the garden, 'plant' them directly in the container, using potting compost.
2 Pack the spaces between with saturated florist's foam. Insert the euphorbia as infill, then the tulips and anemones, informally.

ranging from tots barely 2.5cm (1in) across, to substantial hummocks 15cm (6in) or more across, so the scale of a pot et fleur based on them can vary accordingly.

❖

EASTER DISPLAYS
Lilies, especially *Lilium longiflorum*, either growing or cut, are traditional Easter flowers. Thorny branches evoke Easter's serious

side and combining lilies with thorny branches perfectly captures the symbolism of Easter. As a display, the combination of two such contrasting components is stunning. A good source of thorny branches is the singularly spiky, fascinating *Poncirus trifoliata* with its angular green thorns growing uninterruptedly from its crooked, angled green-barked branches. For a 'softer' interpretation of the death and rebirth theme, combine cut lilies, hazel branches and stag's-horn

LEFT For a softly feminine, sweetly fragrant display with old-fashioned Victorian overtones, combine pots of bedding pansies with cut stems of lilac and periwinkle. Hosta leaves add bold contrast in form, and they are a more interesting alternative to lilac foliage, which is best removed during conditioning.

Plants
HOSTA SIEBOLDIANA
1-3 PANSIES

Cut Flowers and Foliage
8-10 LILACS, BRANCHES STRIPPED OF FOLIAGE
3-4 SPRIGS OF GREATER PERIWINKLE

1 Place the hosta, in its pot, towards the back of a trug and the pansy or pansies, in their pots, in front. If they have been dug up from the garden 'plant' them directly in the container.
2 Pack the spaces between with saturated florist's foam.
3 Insert the lilacs so that they hide the foam and hang over the rim of the container. Finally, add a few sprigs of periwinkle.

RIGHT Quail eggs provide the Easter symbolism for this soft yellow short-term spring display. The natural leaf rosettes of primrose and cowslip provide the foliage, with cut pheasant's-eye narcissus providing height and fragrance. Keep the display cool and, as soon as the flowers fade, plant the primrose and cowslips in the garden.

Plants
PRIMROSE
COWSLIP

Cut Flowers and Foliage
1 BUNCH OF PHEASANT'S-EYE
NARCISSUS
QUAIL EGGS

1 Place the primrose and cowslip, still in their pots, in a deep basket. If dug up from the garden, 'plant' them in the basket.

2 Place a water-filled glass or jar behind the primrose and fill with narcissus.

3 Fill the spaces between the flower pots or rootballs and the jar with damp peat or peat substitute. Arrange the quail eggs decoratively.

fern plants, or arrange cut lilies above a cloud of gypsophila and the velvety leaves of peppermint geranium.

Eggs and bunnies are popular Easter features with children. Small, colourful foil-covered chocolate eggs, or boiled, speckled, pale blue quail eggs can fill a twiggy nest under a 'shrub' of primroses or miniature narcissi in a dish garden, or they can be heaped at the base of growing hyacinths. If you have plenty of eggs they could be placed in an open, lidded wicker box with sprigs of fruit blossom and grape ivy tumbling out. Adding one or more bunnies – china, glass, wicker, stone or wooden – to an ordinary pot et fleur makes it instantly Eastery. They can 'graze' among cut flowers inserted at the base of a holly fern or umbrella plant.

Lemons are associated with the traditional pancakes on Shrove Tuesday, and you can combine a lemon-filled fruit basket with small plants and white or yellowy green Singapore orchids. To create more interesting shapes, halve a few of the lemons and insert sprigs of sweet bay here and there – they are reminiscent of citrus foliage and can remain out of water for days without shrivelling.

The Easter cactus is Brazilian in origin and can actually flower at any time during spring; as Easter itself is a movable feast, the religious, geographical and temporal connection between the two is slender. Young, small plants tend to look ungainly and large, substantial plants are rarely available, so it is best to incorporate one or more small Easter cacti into a pot et fleur. Their high-key, tropical colour looks best with equally intense tones: brassy scarlet or hot pink azaleas, or vermilion or mahogany wallflowers.

SUMMER

❖ ❖ ❖

IN SUMMER ONE IS SPOILED FOR CHOICE, IN TERMS OF BOTH CUT AND
CONTAINERISED MATERIAL. THERE ARE AN ENORMOUS NUMBER OF FLOWERS TO
CUT FROM THE GARDEN, FROM THE PEONIES, DELPHINIUMS, SWEET WILLIAMS
AND IRIS OF EARLY SUMMER TO THE SHASTA DAISIES, PENSTEMONS,
CONEFLOWERS AND CROCOSMIA OF LATE SUMMER. ROSES AND ANNUALS SUCH
AS NASTURTIUMS AND TOBACCO PLANTS PROVIDE A MIXTURE OF SOFT, SUBTLE,
CLEAR AND BRILLIANT TONES ALL SUMMER LONG.

❖ ❖ ❖

RIGHT A bunch of long-stemmed roses may have romantic connotations but visually it is unimaginative and too many rose leaves can look dull. If you have access to garden foliage, you can easily overcome this challenge, but otherwise foliage houseplants, such as the Boston fern, offer a quick solution with a lush, Victorian feel. Although this is a botanical impossibility, since ferns don't flower, the image it creates is charming.

Plants
BOSTON FERN

Cut Flowers and Foliage
10-12 YELLOW ROSES

1 Cut the rose stems to 10cm (4in) long, making the cuts diagonally.
2 Place a small piece of saturated florist's foam in the centre of the fern. Insert the roses in the foam, placing them tightly together to conceal the foundation.
3 Check and adjust the outer fronds, 'fluffing' them up around the roses to hide any foam that remains visible. Keep the display cool, out of direct sunlight, and spray it regularly with water.

In addition to the choice of flowers available from the garden all summer long, there is an equal abundance and variety of deciduous garden foliage – variegated dogwood, abelia, hypericum, weigela and hosta; the golden-leaved varieties of philadelphus, elder and dogwood; the lacy, glaucous foliage of rue; or the rich purple tones of the smoke bush. Use the foliage on its own with house plants to create an unusual pot et fleur, or, more conventionally, add it to the cut-flower component of pot et fleur displays.

Florists and flower stalls reflect this seasonal glut of flowers and foliage, offering 'fresh-from-the-garden' cornflowers, sweet peas, china asters, calendulas, godetias, larkspur and pinks; and their range of foliage is now also rather more imaginative.

In early summer, cow parsley, a prolific hedgerow plant also known as Queen Anne's lace, makes excellent, instant gypsophila-

Purple and yellow may not be an obvious colour combination for interior decor or clothing, but in small doses it can prove eyecatching. The colour of the roses is reflected in the tiny splash of yellow in the centre of each African violet bloom.

Plants
6 AFRICAN VIOLETS

Cut Flowers and Foliage
10-12 YELLOW ROSES

1 Carefully place the African violets, still in their pots, in a basket large enough for the plants to fit in tightly but comfortably.
2 Wedge pieces of saturated florist's foam into any spaces.
3 Cut the rose stems to 7.5-10cm (3-4in) long, making the cuts diagonally.
4 Insert the roses between the African violets, pushing the stems into the florist's foam until the heads are on a level with the African violets.
5 Check the display, adjusting the African violet leaves to conceal any florist's foam.

like filler, its green seed heads equally attractive in late summer pot et fleurs; wild grasses and weeds such as thistle from hedgerow, wood and roadside can create a ruffle or halo for a house plant, inserted in an outer cachepot with the space between tightly packed with saturated florist's foam.

Summer flowers and foliage can have a dual role: blooms of

LEFT Ordinary house plants such as the shrimp plant, dizygotheca and peperomia, with its pale, sinuous flower spikes, make an exotic, opulent display when combined with cut roses and ivy.

Plants
DIZYGOTHECA
VARIEGATED IVY
SHRIMP PLANT
PEPEROMIA

Cut Flowers and Foliage
6 ROSES

1 Place the dizygotheca, still in its pot, at the back of the bowl.
2 Place the shrimp plant to one side, the ivy to the other, and the peperomia, slightly tilted forward to show off its flower spikes, to the front.
3 Pack the spaces between the pots with saturated florist's foam. Wedge it tightly to fit.
4 Cut the roses to varying lengths and insert between the peperomia and ivy to form an irregular, slightly diagonal line. Check that all the florist's foam is concealed, adjusting the foliage as necessary.

heliotrope, ageratum or pelargoniums, for example, can either be cut (the Victorians used them as cut flowers and they are surprisingly long lasting) or used in their pots as the house plant component of pot et fleurs. Scented-leaved pelargoniums, such as the green and white variegated form of the rose-scented *Pelargonium graveolens*, or the velvety grey peppermint 'geranium', *P. tomentosum*, can be taken from plants in need of pruning and displayed as cut foliage, or they can be used in their pots with their roots intact. If they are still turgid when the pot et fleur display is dismantled, the cut stems can be divided into smaller sections of three nodes each which can then be rooted in peat-based potting compost.

Summer also provides the perfect opportunity for blurring the traditional line between house plants and garden plants. Treating everything as raw material results in imaginative, novel displays. As well as conventional house plants and dual-purpose plants such as pelargoniums, busy Lizzies and wax begonias, garden centres often sell garden annuals or tender perennials such as ageratum, petunias, French and African marigolds, stocks and verbena in individual pots, which are ideal for enjoying indoors in a temporary pot et fleur display and then transplanting out to the garden or patio.

❖

ROSES

Their universal availability, broad colour range and sturdy stems make roses excellent pot et fleur material, provided they have steady access to water. If you have no garden but desire a non-florist's effect, buy delicate, multi-stemmed roses. Insert them in a basket of summer-flowering streptocarpus or busy Lizzies and tiny ferns, their pots and potting compost concealed with moss. Or, for a dining-table display, combine them with pots of compact flowering fuchsias, such as those sold for window boxes. Alternatively, antique cups and saucers, each with a posy of roses, can be arranged in the centre of the table around a soup tureen of containerised ferns and cut roses, or pots containing miniature roses.

Almost any foliage or out-of-season flowering house plant, provided it is healthy looking, can be enlivened with cut roses. If you can't be bothered creating an all-in-one arrangement in a single cachepot or basket, simply display roses in close proximity: place them singly in tumblers or wine glasses on either side of the plant for classical symmetry, or encircling the plant if it is to be seen from all round, as when placed on a coffee table. Try inserting a few sprigs of foliage from the house plant with the roses. If the house plant is displayed against a wall, the roses can be placed in a concealed container behind the plant – especially effective with house plants that have fountain-like or upright growth.

❖

THREE WAYS WITH STORE-BOUGHT ROSES

Florists' roses, once an expensive, seasonal token of love, are now a reasonably priced, universally available, year-round commodity, rather like the floral equivalent of bananas. Nonetheless, there is always a thrill in buying or receiving a bunch of roses, and displaying them in a pot et fleur is a lovely way to enjoy them.

The length of stem, which can be up to 1m (39in), is part of the cost of roses, so, unless you specifically want a tall display, those with modest stem lengths are fine. As well as conventional hybrid teas, florists sell spray roses with several heads per stem, mini, or sweetheart, roses with perfect but diminutive blooms, and loose- rather than tight-budded varieties for a 'fresh-from-the-garden' look. If the bunch includes a few sprigs of gypsophila, try to incorporate them into the display. The arrangements shown on pages 48, 49 and 50 are based on one bunch of roses and ordinary houseplants, but you can vary the choice and colours of roses and plants to suit taste and availability.

❖

ANNUALS, BIENNIALS AND BEDDING PLANTS

For small pot et fleurs needing a splash of colour you can buy annuals, biennials or bedding plants in pots, but to save money, and for large displays, buy annuals in trays, or flats, and pot up individually for pot et fleurs. The extras can go straight into the garden, window boxes or hanging baskets, or you can split them with friends.

RIGHT Here, a trug is filled with an informal mixture of garden-centre plants and old-fashioned garden flowers. Exact numbers are not given for the flowers, since the proportions are less important than a generous over-all effect, which can be judged by eye.

Plants
MARGUERITE
STRAWBERRY

Cut Flowers and Foliage
KNAPWEED
MASTERWORT
HARDY GERANIUM
BUDDLEIA
LAVENDER

1 Position the marguerite and strawberry plants in the trug, with the marguerite providing the central height and the strawberry plant arching over the rim. If the strawberry plant is taken from the garden, pot it up a day or two beforehand, water thoroughly and leave to recover in a shaded place.
2 Place a shallow, water-filled container near the front of the trug, strip the lower leaves off the cut flowers and lay them loosely in the trug, so that their stems are submerged and their heads over-hang the trug rim. If using cut flowers with rigid stems, saturated florist's foam can be substituted.

Visit garden centres and see what is available that pleases you and matches your decor.

Fill a large, low container with wax begonia, French marigold, golden-leaved dwarf feverfew or lobelia bedding plants, and create a central, fountain-like display of toning or contrasting cut flowers or of cool, green foliage.

Miniature standard 'marguerites' (former members of the *Chrysanthemum* genus, now re-classified as *Argyranthemum*) are woody-stemmed, tender perennials sold and treated as annuals. They can form the tree-like focal point, singly or in a row, of a pot et fleur, 'underplanted' with cut sprigs of ageratum or garden pinks studded in moss. Alternatively, make a 'lawn' of lobelia under 'trees' made of branches of small-leaved shrubs.

LEFT Using a mixture of house plants, garden plants and cut flowers in tints or shades of the same colour can produce a variety of startlingly original combinations, some with a longer shelf life than others. Here, a tropical dracaena and some petunias are combined as the foundation of a short-term pot et fleur, created in an elegant window-box type trough.

RIGHT Here, the cut flowers are spiky in outline, their height equalling that of the dracaena. Astilbes can be short-lived as cut flowers, but will certainly survive a summer lunch or evening party.

Plants
DRACAENA
2-4 PETUNIAS

Cut Flowers and Foliage
6-10 LARKSPUR
6-10 ASTILBE, EITHER PINK OR MIXED PINK AND WHITE

1 Place the petunias and dracaena, still in their pots, in the outer container, with the dracaena at the centre back.
2 Pack the spaces between the pots with saturated florist's foam, wedged securely.
3 Insert the larkspur and astilbe into the florist's foam, slightly angling the outer flowers to overhang the container.

The campanula is another tender perennial often used as an annual. A big basket of blue-, lilac- or white-flowered varieties, or a mixture, needs no adornment, but you could combine them with cut foliage such as the boldly green-and-white striped, sword-like leaves of *Iris foetidissima* 'Variegata', or any of the variegated hostas, to balance the campanulas' own sparse leaves, and to contrast with their somewhat sprawling growth habit.

Mass the exotic, tropical-looking blooms of annual schizanthus, or poor man's orchid, sold in individual pots, with cut stems of globe thistles or sea holly for contrast. Some annuals such as cockscomb and Prince of Wales feather are curiously formal and artificial looking, perhaps better suited to pot et fleurs than to growing in today's informal, natural-looking gardens. Combine them with equally exotic-looking house plants such as crotons or multi-colour coleus, or garden foliage such as multi-coloured phormiums.

The curved spikes of bells of Ireland are perhaps better known in their preserved, ivory white form than their fresh, sharp green form. Use the latter to enhance climbing philodendrons such as *P. domesticum*, or the large-scale, fountain-like *P. bipinnatifidum*, neither of which blooms in cultivation.

The huge, intact stems of love-lies-bleeding, especially in its green form, are splendid for adding grand-scale verticality to house plant groups. Remove the leaves before adding to the arrangement; the hanging panicles of tassel-like flowers will dry naturally in situ, and can then be used for dried-flower displays.

❖

GARDEN PERENNIALS

As with bedding plants destined for the garden, containerised summer perennials can be used in temporary pot et fleurs, then planted out. The recent trend in marketing specimen-sized perennials in full flower or leaf provides excellent raw material for 'one-night-stands' – large-scale pot et fleurs for dinner party centrepieces, for example. When you think that cut flowers are sooner or later (often sooner) discarded, the extra expense of buying plants in flower is more than compensated for by their potential to provide cut flowers for many years. And some plants we now consider as strictly garden plants – astilbes, for example, and box elder – were used by Victorians as house plants, so there is a historical precedent. Just keep them cool and make sure that the potting compost is damp, but not soggy.

There are too many summer perennials to list individually, but certain types of perennials, such as those belonging to the *Compositae*

RIGHT Blue and white china, such as traditional Willow Garden and Oriental Pheasant patterns, Italian spongeware and Delft, has long been popular. A mixture of blue and white containers can provide inspiration for a pot et fleur display, though matching the distinct, rich blue of some china can be quite a challenge.

Plants
1-2 CAMPANULA CARPATICA
1-2 CAMPANULA CARPATICA 'ALBA'

Cut Flowers and Foliage
8-10 AGERATUM
8-10 SCABIOUS
1 STEM OF GYPSOPHILA
1 BUNCH OF SEA LAVENDER

1 Strip the lower leaves off the ageratum and place in a water-filled jug.
2 Cut the scabious stems slightly shorter than the ageratum and insert in another water-filled container with the gypsophila sprigs.
3 Place the campanulas, still in their pots, in a bowl, and pack the space between with saturated florist's foam.
4 Insert sprigs of sea lavender in tight clumps between the plants, to conceal the florist's foam, and here and there in the middle.
You can insert some sprigs in the pots themselves, since sea lavender dries naturally.

family, with typical daisy flowers, have summery overtones. Daisy blooms range from charming ox-eye wild daisies and chamomile to shasta daisies, exotically coloured osteospermums and unusual blue kingfisher daisies. (The latter two could equally be listed under annuals, since both are frost tender and, except in mild gardens, treated as annual bedding.) Single, white chrysanthemums from florists make an acceptable commercial substitute. Later in summer, there are asters, rudbeckias and pyrethrums. Use a big, old kangaroo vine or grape ivy as the backdrop for a cut flower display based on daisies, and encircle the container or interwine the flower stems with trailing vine. Alternatively, make a 'field' of cut daisies in a shallow basket of moss, surrounded by a rim of trailing lobelia plants.

Spiky flowers are another summer treat: the early summer spikes of foxgloves, lupins, campanulas and delphiniums and later summer spikes of red hot pokers and mullein. Combine them with the

LEFT AND RIGHT Streptocarpus, or Cape primrose, is a beautiful South African house plant, with tubular flowers in shades of pink, purple, magenta, rose, blue or white in summer or autumn, carried elegantly above rosettes of strap-shaped leaves. A favourite for shady windowsills in country cottages, some varieties have blooms with contrasting throats or pencilling. Here, the plants form the basis of toning pot et fleurs.

Plants
2 CAPE PRIMROSES

Cut Flowers and Foliage
10-12 CAMPANULAS
8-10 EUSTOMAS

1 Place the Cape primroses, still in their pots, side by side in a rectangular container.
2 Pack the spaces between with saturated florist's foam, wedged tightly to fit.
3 Insert the campanulas and eustomas amongst the Cape primroses, placing taller stems at the back for a front-facing display, as here, and shorter ones towards the front.
4 Check the arrangement regularly and remove the faded florets, as this will encourage all the buds to open.

naturally arching stems of various asparagus ferns, or any of the upright, cane begonias such as the angel's wing begonia. Cut stems of Solomon's seal, which combine verticality with a gracefully arching tip, can hover over a dish garden of gold, green and variegated varieties of baby's tears, or of Persian violets.

For short-lived displays indoors, use hostas cut or as pot plants. Set a good-sized plant, its foliage free from slug holes, in moss

59

RIGHT A completely different, more sculptural effect from the previous arrangement is achieved by substituting love-in-a-mist and thistles for the softer-looking campanulas and eustomas.

Plants
2 CAPE PRIMROSES

Cut Flowers and Foliage
1 LARGE BUNCH OF LOVE-IN-A-MIST
8-10 THISTLES

1 Place the Cape primroses, still in their pots, side by side in a rectangular container.
2 Pack the spaces between with saturated florist's foam, wedged tightly to fit.
3 Insert the love-in-a-mist and thistles amongst the Cape primroses, placing taller stems at the back for a front-facing display, as here, and shorter ones towards the front. Allow the flowers in the front to overspill the rim.

over saturated florist's foam and stud it with short-stemmed summer flowers. Alternatively, you could use it as a foreground for lilies, or for a collection of cut ornamental miniature pineapple tops or proteas. Cut hosta leaves can form a stage setting for a jewel-like house plant such as a cactus in flower. Newly emerging hosta foliage can be difficult to condition successfully; submerging it in water overnight before arranging may help.

Play the game of providing out-of-season, flowering house plants with flowers of the appropriate colour. For example, match yellow day lilies, goldenrod or achillea with a zebra plant, or use orange lilies to replace the spring blooms of *Clivia miniata*. Alternatively, use blooms of another colour or, for an amusing effect, mixed colours. Wire small blocks of saturated florist's foam to the trunks of tree-like house plants such as dracaena, false aralia, umbrella tree or Yucca plant; insert flowers and foliage into the foam to create pot et fleurs with a hint of fantasy. Or for a quick fix, simply insert big stems of fennel into the cachepots of palms or weeping figs. At the other end of the scale, combine delicate columbine blooms with the equally delicate maidenhair fern house plants.

❖

BULBS
Although spring is the season for bulbs en masse, lilies in pots are too good, and too available, to ignore for use in summer pot et fleurs. Display them with cut foliage in glass tanks; conceal their pots and the cut-foliage containers or foundations with a layer of fresh and dried moss, bark, shells, marbles or pebbles.

For high drama, combine cut stems of the ornamental onion or bolted leek flower heads from the vegetable garden with large-scale house plant foliage such as fatsia or fatshedera, and limes, lemons and starfruit impaled on canes stuck into florist's foam.

The greenish white, star-shaped blooms of star of Bethlehem, a relative of long-lasting chincherinchee, are equally long-lasting when cut. A wildflower of grassy places, stars of Bethlehem are lovely in rough, grassy wild gardens. Tuck the cut flowers into low-growing,

sprawling house plants such as variegated buffalo grass, and conceal the water receptacles among the house plant foliage. Or make concentric cirles of tightly packed cut flowers – an outer circle of star of Bethlehem round an inner circle of sweet Williams, for example, with a small, compact house plant forming the 'bull's eye'.

❖

Climbing and Trailing Plants

Trailing or climbing summer annuals include the communal garden nasturtium, the tender black-eyed Susan, Chilean glory flower with its racemes of orange-red tubular flowers, and morning glory. All are available, often trained up tripods, from larger garden centres. Use them as they are, or gently untwine them and drape them round the rim of a basket or shallow dish, or coil them round the handle of a basket filled with cut flowers. Passionflowers in bloom are often sold with their stems wrapped round a hoop. Cape leadwort with its clear, sky-blue blooms, is also sold this way. These can look awkward on their own, especially if the circle is wonky, but they make excellent components for pot et fleurs, with the central space filled with cut flowers.

Trailing plants for hanging baskets are in vogue, and sophisticated alternatives to the traditional lobelia, nasturtium and ivy-leaved pelargonium can be used in pot et fleurs. One of the most charming is the Australian or ivy-leaved violet, with its diminutive purple and white blooms. Only 2.5-5cm (1-2in) high, its trailing stolons form tiny plantets along its nodes, each of which can root and form an independent plant. Another is *Diascia barberiae* 'Rose Queen', with its trailing stems and upright spikes of pale pink, lipped blooms.

These, and others, are conveniently sold in packs of six tiny pots, like beer or eggs! Place one in each corner of a square wicker basket filled with a summery cut-flower display, and spread their trails over the crisp linen, glass or mirrored surface of a dining or coffee table. If the basket has a handle, twine trails up the handle from each end, to meet in the middle. Do this well before the display is needed, to allow the plants to 'settle', and keep them cool until needed.

LEFT For a sweetly scented display with overtly romantic appeal, try combining the waxy white blooms of stephanotis, a tropical climber traditionally trained round a support of canes, with a mixture of summer-flowering perennials and shrubs. This pot et fleur would be ideal for a wedding or christening.

Plants

STEPHANOTIS

Cut Flowers and Foliage

6-8 ROSES
2-3 PEONIES
3-4 SPRIGS OF ORANGE BLOSSOM
3-4 SPRIGS OF DEUTZIA

1 Place the stephanotis, still in its pot, at the back of a moss-lined basket or similar container.
2 Pack the remainder of the container with saturated florist's foam.
3 Cut the rose and peony stems to several lengths, then insert the blooms to form a rough V-shape, with a concentration of blooms in the point of the V.
4 Insert the orange blossom and deutzia sprigs to fill out the base, conceal the florist's foam and soften the silhouette.

RIGHT Concentric circles of tightly packed house plants and flowers or foliage are a simple formula for success. A polka-dot plant is the 'bull's-eye' for this display, made in a ring of florist's foam. It is surrounded by chincherinchees, with an outer ring of sweet Williams. Whether cut or bought in bud, sweet Williams and chincherinchees are very long lasting.

Plants
1 OR MORE SMALL POLKA-DOT
PLANTS

Cut Flowers and Foliage
12-15 CHINCHERINCHEES
18-24 SWEET WILLIAMS

1 Place the polka-dot plant or plants, still potted, in the centre of a florist's foam ring or circular container filled with blocks of foam cut and wedged tightly to fit.
2 Cut the chincherinchee stems to 7.5-10cm (3-4in) long and insert the flowers in a tight circle around the plants, coming roughly level with, or just below, the plants.
3 Cut the sweet William stems to a similar length and use them to make an outer circle as above but slightly lower than the chincherinchees and covering the sides of the florist's foam.

FRUITS AND VEGETABLES

For many people, summer means strawberries. Impale firm but ripe strawberries on cocktail sticks or short lengths of plastic-coated wires in a summer display of small foliage house plants, cut daisies, roses and lady's mantle. Alternatively, gently dig up a couple of plants in flower and fruit, or buy them at the garden centre, and pot them up for pot et fleurs. Place them in a trug interspersed with cut flowers; any runners can be artfully arranged to trail over the table, or even down the sides, of a white tablecloth.

Miniature tomato plants make jovial pot et fleurs. Combine them with African or French marigolds, as often happens in the garden or greenhouse, where the marigolds reputedly repel insect pests from the tomatoes.

Pile slender courgettes, together with their billowy yellow blooms, radially in a basket or large dish, around pots of either African marigolds, whose huge heads seem more suited to theatrical displays than gardens, or the more modest blooms of French marigolds. Use cut ivy sprigs or nasturtiums as the third, unifying component, or simply omit the marigolds and create a fountain of fern or tiny palm and cut nasturtiums in the centre of the courgettes.

Grapes as props in cut-flower or pot et fleur displays can have dusty, self-conscious overtones, reminiscent of Fifties flower arrangements, and their being available all year round robs them of some of their original, summery connotations. Even so, grapes piled high round a central slipper orchid or moth orchid look good. Grape foliage, whether from fruiting or ornamental vines, makes a handsome addition to a pot et fleur, with or without its fruit.

Red currants are jewel-like in transparency and colour; cherries are their opaque equivalent. Festoon foliage house plants with pairs or triplets of cherries, sprigs of red currant, or, for a more subtle effect, black currant or opalescent pearly berries of white currant, and set them in a nest of cut flowers. Alternatively, include whole branches in pot et fleurs. Prepare the stems in the usual way, but if the leaves start to wilt, strip them and just use the berry-laden branches.

RIGHT You can interpret the term 'pot et fleur' as loosely as you like. Here, a bunch of red roses, a bunch of sea lavender and an alpine campanula are displayed separately but close enough together to still form an instant pot et fleur. The sea lavender can dry in situ as a long-term ingredient for future pot et fleurs, and after the display the campanula can be planted out in the garden. For this arrangement, there can be as much creativity involved in choosing the containers as there is in choosing their contents.

Plants
CAMPANULA CARPATICA 'ALBA'

Cut Flowers and Foliage
1 BUNCH OF SEA LAVENDER
12-18 LONG-STEMMED FLORISTS'
ROSES

1 Place the campanula, still in its pot, in an attractive cachepot.
2 Strip the lower leaves from the roses and place them in a jug. Place the sea lavender in a separate container.
3 Arrange the three components, with the tallest element – the roses – at the back.

Use whole stalks of sweetcorn, especially the variegated forms, as outsized, ornamental grass backdrops to a large pot et fleur; huge stalks of globe artichoke can perform a similar task. Cut short, one thistle can provide the focal point for a mixed basket of house plants: choose house plants with a hint of purple, such as wandering sailor, the blue-flowered torch plant or the purple velvet plant, to match the purple thistle.

On a smaller scale, festoon boring house plants with strands of purple-podded varieties of climbing or dwarf French beans, or pea stems, complete with curly tendrils, blooms and pods. First remove their leaves, which would otherwise wilt.

Fruit and vegetables displayed with cut surfaces are liable to rot, especially in a warm room and will need to be replaced. Even if they are left intact, ripening fruits and vegetables release ethylene gas, which shortens the life of certain blooms if they are in close proximity, such as irises and freesias. If placed in a cool room, however, pot et fleurs comprising cut and growing foliage and uncut fruit and vegetables can last for a week or more.

❖

QUICK FIXES
Though available from florists all year round, gypsophila is a sun- and chalk-loving garden plant and is always summery in its connotations. Like the carnations to which it is related, gypsophila is long suffering out of water, and, once cut, dries naturally on the branch. Sticking sprigs of gypsophila into a mixed house plant dish garden converts it to an instant pot et fleur. You can keep the sprigs short so that they hover just above the moss, or use them full length, creating a two-tier display, like the inspirational, floating light bulb that appears above the heads of cartoon figures.

Cow parsley, if you live in the country or have access to it during weekend outings, is a super alternative to gypsophila; as are the slightly larger blooms of pink or white soapwort. Lady's mantle has more prominent stems in relation to the tiny blooms but they are still useful as an airy filler of an unusual acid green.

WATER GARDEN POT ET FLEURS

You can play this two ways: either put house plants which need constantly wet conditions, such as *Acorus gramineus* 'Variegatus' or *Cyperus alternifolius*, in a large, opaque container of water with cut flowers and foliage; or create a shallow indoor ornamental pond in a transparent glass bowl. For the latter, borrow floating aquatic plants, such as water hyacinths or fairy moss with trailing roots, from an ornamental garden pond. Even the dreaded duckweed, scourge of garden ponds, can make a velvety, surface carpet, punctuated with floating heads of gerberas; each dot-like duckweed is a plant in itself, thus qualifying the display as a genuine pot et fleur. For verticality, impale tall stems of iris or arum lily on a heavy metal pin holder, Japanese style; the pin holder can form part of the display.

❖

Summer Containers

Cachepots and outer containers, being non-living, are by definition non-seasonal, but nothing says 'summer' quite so effectively as baskets and trugs made from natural materials, such as wicker, wooden slats or vine stems. Summer pot et fleurs can take the form of playful puns: baskets with sides made of tightly packed dried lavender stems, for example, can hold a mixture of containerised, small summer flowering or foliage plants or herbs, spiked with freshly cut lavender, or even small pots of dwarf lavender, set in moss, with lavender potpourri sprinkled over the surface as a finishing touch. Lastly, coconuts and cucurbits such as marrows and melons have long been scooped out as containers for flowers but they can also hold small house plants as well.

LEFT A tall, narrow wire container holding a clear glass tumbler and a shallow wire basket form the basis for this display of lady's mantle, petunias, gloxinias and throatwort. Lady's mantle is invaluable for providing gypsophila-like 'fluff', but with more colour and seasonal character. It is now being grown commercially for florists, so it's worth asking your florist to stock it, if they don't already.

Plants
GLOXINIA
PETUNIA

Cut Flowers and Foliage
3 THROATWORTS
2 LARGE BUNCHES OF LADY'S MANTLE

1 Insert one bunch of lady's mantle in the tall container, then insert the throatworts in the centre. Adjust the lady's mantle to form an informal ruffle, raised at the back and dipped in the front.
2 Place the gloxinia, still in its pot, in the back of a moss-lined basket, and the petunia, still in its pot, in front.
3 Pack the spaces between with saturated florist's foam. Create a similar ruffle of lady's mantle, filling the spaces between the two plants.

AUTUMN

❖ ❖ ❖

AUTUMN COLOURS RANGE FROM SUBTLE TO FIERY, BUT THE EMPHASIS IS ON

THE WARM YELLOWS, ORANGES, RUSSETS AND REDS. DRIED FLOWERS PLAY AS

COMMANDING A ROLE AS FRESH ONES, PARTICULARLY LATER IN THE SEASON,

AND FRUITS, VEGETABLES AND BERRIES, BOTH ORNAMENTAL AND EDIBLE,

PROVIDE RICH PICKINGS FOR POT ET FLEURS.

❖ ❖ ❖

Right Calla lilies, or arum lilies, and a leafy rex begonia make a quick and surprisingly sophisticated arrangement. Oyster mushrooms, repeating the lilies' glowing colour and sinuous curves, add an autumnal touch and complete the vignette. Oyster mushrooms grow wild on trees such as birch and elder and are also available from specialist gourmet foodshops and, unceremoniously shrink-wrapped in plastic punnets, from the larger supermarket chains.

Plants
BEGONIA REX

Cut Flowers and Funghi
12-15 CALLA LILIES
1 PUNNET OF OYSTER MUSHROOMS

1 Thoroughly water the begonia, then place it in a bowl deep enough to conceal its pot. Pack the space between the pot and the bowl with pieces of saturated florist's foam.
2 Place the oyster mushrooms in a similar, or contrasting, bowl.
3 Cut the stems of the lilies so that the blooms extend slightly above the house plant foliage. Insert individual stems in the florist's foam and damp potting compost in twos and threes.

For pot et fleur raw material, autumn is unrivalled. Its cooler temperatures and shorter days can bring a most vivid display of garden colour. Especially in North America, the rich hues of autumn leaves intensify the already rich palette of dahlias, gladioli, red-hot pokers, chrysanthemums and Michaelmas daisies. Often, the cooler temperatures can give a second lease of life to roses, fuchsias, bedding plants and annuals, all of which can look a little tatty in the heat of late summer, and herbaceous perennials, such as delphiniums, may produce a second flush of flowers.

Later in autumn, as frost threatens, cutting flowers from the garden for pot et fleurs is no longer constrained by the fear of 'robbing the garden' for indoor decoration. In late autumn, too, the psychological need for bright, cheerful colour indoors increases – the connection, long suspected, between some depressions and low sunlight levels has now been scientifically established.

The late summer/early autumn fruit and vegetable harvest provides an equally rich source of pot et fleur 'props': yellow, red, purple-black, white and green bell peppers; purple and unusual white

LEFT Pears, dried flowers, dried grass and a variegated *hebe* are used to create an autumnal effect. This particular *hebe* is ideal for a window box or as the focal point in a winter hanging basket.

Plants
VARIEGATED *HEBE*

*Dried Flowers,
Seedpods and Fruit*
DRIED FLOWERS AND GRASSES
PEARS

1 Make small, graded bunches of the dried grass and dried flowers and tie them tightly with florist's wire. Cut the stems to an even length, to come well above the rim of the basket.
2 Using a hot glue gun or quick-drying glue, fix alternating bunches of grass and flowers round the basket. Wind some raffia around the grass and tie it in a bow at the front of the basket.
3 Carefully place the hebe, still in its pot, in the basket and position the pears to one side.

aubergines; apples, pears, plums and grapes in a variety of rich hues. Impaled on florist's stub wires, dowels, bamboo canes or branches and inserted into the potting compost, or heaped round the base of a pot et fleur, they add to the seasonal effect. So-called 'ornamental' berries, many of which – for example berberis, rose hips, elderberries, rowan and crab-apple – actually make delicious preserves, are also rich pickings for pot et fleurs.

Yellow, orange, red, russet, purple and brown are seen as autumnal colours, and a touch of one or more of those can be combined with a seasonless, plain foliage house plant such as ivy, fern or spider plant to create an autumnal pot et fleur. These colours, however, may not suit a particular decor, and many splendid autumn garden flowers, from fuchsia-pink Guernsey lilies and kaffir lilies to brilliant blue gentians and monkshoods, defy any such colour rules. Likewise certain house plants – the pale or deep blue tubular flowers of Cape primrose, for example, and the summery blue, starry-flowered campanula – bloom well into autumn.

Although, for ease of reading, the text below is divided into the various components of autumnal pot et fleurs, in reality the divisions are obscured. A dried thistle head, for example, is both a flower and a seedpod; and pot et fleurs, like good antipasti, can contain a little of several contrasting 'ingredients'.

❖

DRIED FLOWERS

Drying flowers and seed heads is an ornamental variation on the seasonal theme of harvesting, preserving and storing food crops for winter use. Newly dried flowers are at their brightest in the autumn, and, as with freshly cut flowers, they offer instant colour and variety to foliage or out-of-season flowering house plants. With no need for water, the stems can be inserted directly into a cachepot or into florist's foam or crumpled wire mesh within the cachepot. Alternatively, they can be carefully inserted in the plant's potting compost or placed amongst its foliage.

A florist's mixed bunch of dried flowers can look sparse and

LEFT The simplest and most time-saving pot et fleur of all – a parlour palm flanked by cut flowers and foliage of constrasting shapes and colours. On the left is a bunch of ramrod-straight purple allium, and on the right, the little yellow bobbles of Mimosa.

Plants
PARLOUR PALM

Cut Flowers and Foliage
ALLIUM
MIMOSA

1 Re-pot the parlour palm, if necessary, in a terracotta pot.
2 Place the allium and the mimosa in vases with plenty of water, remembering to strip off the lower leaves of the mimosa so that they are not covered in water. Arrange the vases so that they flank the parlour palm, creating a triangular shape.

stiff displayed on its own – the drying process gets rid of most of the leaves and results in poker-straight stems. Intermingled with house plant foliage in a pot et fleur, however, the dried flowers become altogether more attractive.

A dried flower pot et fleur display will last, theoretically, as long as the house plant does, but in practice it is nice to ring the changes. If they become dusty, dried flowers look dismal. You can blow the dust off with an air-filled aerosol, as used by professional photographers, but if the flowers are also faded, discard them or save them for spray-painting for Christmas.

Many naturally dried flowers lack the intense, clear colour of fresh blooms but dyed, dried flowers are available, in clear and subtle colours, with varying degrees of naturalness. Very often it is only the dye extending down the stems that gives the game away. The house plant foliage or cut foliage can conceal this, or the artificiality can be accepted at face value.

Combining dried flowers with house plants can take various forms. A dried-flower arrangement made on florist's foam can be placed on the potting compost of large, bare-stemmed plants such as Madagascar dragon tree, parlour palm or European fan palm. Further dried material can be added and a few of the outer stems angled down to overhang the rim of the pot and conceal any florist's foam. If wished, as a short-term finishing touch, cover the remaining exposed surface with dried reindeer moss.

Alternatively, dried flowers can be built up on a ring of crumpled wire mesh wound round the stem of a large house plant. Try not to wet it when watering the plant.

Small house plants can be placed in the centre of a horizontally displayed dried-flower ring, using the height of the dried flowers to conceal the pots. Or you can decorate the rim or entire outer surface of a moss basket with dried flowers, then fill it with foliage house plants.

Since a dried-flower display is lightweight enough not to cause damage, it can rest on top of a trailing plant. For an instant pot et fleur, place a pomander of dried rosebuds on a hanging basket

ABOVE AND RIGHT Several of these modest, small-scale *Peperomia caperata* can form the background for a stunning seasonal pot et fleur. Rich purple berberis and Venetian sumach foliage from the garden and blackberries from the hedgerow provide the dark green perperomias with subtle contrast and autumnal overtones. Venetian sumach needs special conditioning: dip the cut ends briefly in boiling water, then submerge the whole stem in water for several hours to prevent it from wilting.

Plants
2 PEPEROMIAS

Cut Flowers and Berries
8-10 BRANCHES OF BERBERIS
6-8 BRANCHES OF VENETIAN
SUMACH
4-6 SPRIGS OF BLACKBERRY

1 Place the peperomias, still in their pots, in a basket, and pack the surrounding space with saturated florist's foam.
2 Remove the lowest leaves from the berberis and Venetian sumach branches, and insert the stems in the florist's foam, around and between the plants. Ensure that some overhang the rim of the container.
3 Remove the lowest leaves from the blackberry stems and insert them in the display at intervals, taking care to fill any gaps.

filled with a colourful display such as rat's-tail cactus, the purple passion vine, the goldfish plant or hearts entangled. To keep the lower flowers off the potting compost surface, you can impale the pomander on a short dowel, which is then pushed into the pot.

Be creative with dried-flower trees. Fill a wide basket with miniature cacti, raising their pots if necessary on florist's foam, crumpled newspaper or wire mesh, and use a small dried-flower tree or trees

RIGHT Simple solutions are often the most refreshing and memorable. This trio of wicker baskets contains dried love-in-a-mist seedpods, ripe pears and a small *Hebe* 'Autumn Glory'. After the display is over, plant the hebe out in a sunny spot in well-drained soil or a well-crocked container.

Plants
HEBE 'AUTUMN GLORY'

Seedpods and Fruit
1 LARGE BUNCH OF LOVE-IN-A-MIST SEEDPODS
RIPE PEARS

1 Cut the seedpod stems to varying heights, but mainly twice as tall as the basket. Pack tightly into the container until evenly full all the way round.
2 Place the hebe, still in its pot, in another basket, and put the pears in a third. If you do not have quite enough pears to fill up the basket, you can rest them on crumpled newspaper.

as focal points for the 'forest', adding a temporary, smooth top dressing of gravel chippings. These trees also go with leafy trailing plants such as ribbon grass. Combine large dried-flower trees with large house plants: specimen weeping figs, for example, or a multi-stemmed variegated song of India.

Tuck huge dried hydrangea heads and Australian honeysuckle blooms into a large out-of-flower *clivia*, variegated pineapple plant or orchid cactus. For a miniature pot et fleur, the tiny blooms of dried glixia or grass daisy come in many colours and can be inserted in almost any small-scale house plant to add an airy 'halo' of colour. Though fiddly and time consuming, it is a simple exercise which gives sophisticated results; try it with an out-of-flower jungle cactus such as the Easter cactus, or with the ready-made posy base of a mature piggyback plant.

If, in the course of arranging dried flowers for conventional displays, you break a few stems – often the case with dried roses and helichrysums – save the flower heads for resting in the centre of low-growing foliage plants such as the aluminium plant or the peanut cactus for diminutive table-top displays.

House plants with especially autumnal tones for complementing dried (and seasonal fresh!) flowers include *Coleus blumei* hybrids and *Begonia rex* hybrids in golden, orange, coppery, russet or wine-red tones; copper leaf; boat lily; crotons and variegated forms of the ti plant. Combine golden-yellow dried strawflowers, dried mimosa and dried goldenrod with a yellow-variegated croton or coleus; or deep-red varieties of dried cockscomb, strawflower and dried kangaroo paw with reddish-purple rex begonia, croton, ti plant or coleus.

❖

FRESH AUTUMN FLOWERS
Gladioli may be a joke in sophisticated circles, but in autumn they are cheap and widely available. Their awkward shape and sword-like leaves (the Latin word *gladius* means sword) can be visually softened by using them, together with glycerined chestnut or birch leaves, as the backdrop for a group of large bromeliads such as *Nidularium*

fulgens. If you have a specimen tree ivy or Swiss cheese plant trained up a moss pole, arrange the gladioli tightly and vertically around the base, to give the impression of a flowering climber.

Use the soft brown leaves of the eyelash begonia as a foil to the orange sprays of montbretia, red pompon dahlias, Peruvian lilies or reddish-brown stonecrops. You can use fresh stonecrops as you would dried flowers, since they air dry naturally.

80

LEFT Proteas are the national flower of South Africa, though they are widely grown elsewhere, including Australia, and come in many forms. Here they are combined with banksias, gold- and bronze-sprayed globe artichoke hearts and glycerined beech leaves. Although exotic items like these can be expensive, they can be reused indefinitely and the dried and glycerined material needs neither potting compost nor water.

Plants

2 PEPEROMIAS

Dried Flowers and Foliage

2 BANKSIAS

4 PROTEAS

5 SPRAYED ARTICHOKE HEARTS

GLYCERINED BEECH BRANCHES

1 Place the peperomias, still in their pots, in a basket, and pack the surrounding space with dry florist's foam.

2 Cut the glycerined beech branches into manageable sprigs and insert, angled slightly downwards, in the florist's foam, to overhang the basket rim.

3 Insert the banksias towards the back of the display and the proteas towards the front.

4 Fill a smaller, adjacent basket with 2 or 3 artichokes, and place the remaining ones nearby to balance the display.

The climbing shrub cape leadwort flowers in late summer and autumn. Though it eventually grows 3m (10ft) or more high as a conservatory plant, small, young plants are usually trained round a hoop. Use one as the focal point of an autumnal display with blue Michaelmas daisies, the blue berries of berberis and cut branches of the shrubby veronica, *Hebe* 'Autumn Glory'.

The velvety tassel flowers of love-lies-bleeding are mostly crimson except in the variety 'Viridis' where they are green. Though usually sold on uniformly short lengths of stem, one tassel per stem, whole plants are magnificent, multibranched, up to 1m (3ft) or more high and worth growing if you have the space. Cut off the roots, strip the leaves, and insert one or more in a large cachepot – a basket, perhaps, or old wooden trunk – with a specimen house plant such as weeping fig, umbrella tree, false castor oil plant or African lime. You can do the same with carthamus, usually sold in small, 'polite' bunches but magnificent as a 1m (3ft) high multistemmed plant. Both air dry naturally, so can be used without water.

Mixed edible flowers – nasturtiums, borage, pansies, calendulas – are surprisingly inexpensive, sold in plastic packages in the salad departments of larger supermarkets. For a delicate, low-level pot et fleur, set a group of small foliage house plants in a basket, pack the space between with crumpled newspaper or florist's foam, and cover the entire surface with fresh bun moss. At the last moment, arrange the edible flowers on top, face up.

❖

DRIED SEEDPODS AND GRAINS

Seedpods range from the cottage-garden biennial honesty to globular poppies in beige or dyed colours, the spiky, bauble-like globe thistle, dyer's greenwood and statuesque teasel.

Insert several bare stems of one type of seedpod in the potting compost of a foliage house plant so that the pods hover above the plant. Match the scale of one to the other: the small, steely-blue thistles of sea holly, for example, rising above glaucous blue echeveria rosettes or velvety-white *Tradescantia sillamontana*; or queen's tears with love-

ABOVE AND LEFT Terracotta pots filled with dried roses are pretty and easy to construct. Simply pack a pot with dry florist's foam, shorten the stems of your dried roses and insert them in a closely-packed bunch, then cover the foundation with sphagnum moss. The addition of miniature ferns in tiny terracotta urns makes an appealing small-scale display.

Plants
6 MINIATURE FERNS

Dried Flowers
ROSE-FILLED TERRACOTTA POT

1 Re-pot the ferns in terracotta containers of a similar size to the roses' container.
2 Arrange the ferns in a circle with the roses in the middle.

in-a-mist seedpods or the virtually black petal-less seed heads of dried coneflower.

Dried grains such as barley, wheat, rye and oats and ornamental grasses such as fescues, hare's tail grass and quaking grass are useful for adding a sense of movement to pot et fleurs. They can appear explosive, however, if they radiate individually and at random from an imaginary central point. Florists often wire ornamental grains and grasses into tight bunches before use; in any case, try to group them into clusters or large solid vertical clumps: an upright

RIGHT For adding instant floral interest and colour to a trained ivy 'topiary' ring you can attach dried roses, using fine florist's wire. Here, the ivy frames the rose-filled terracotta pot and the tray provides a unifying base.

Plants

IVY TRAINED ROUND A RING

Dried Flowers

6 DRIED ROSES
ROSE-FILLED TERRACOTTA POT

1 Cut the stems off the six roses, leaving a stub 15mm (¹/₂in) long.
2 If wished, tease out a few ivy stems from the ring, to create a sense of movement and informality.
3 Using florist's wire, attach the roses, evenly spaced apart, to the ivy ring. Place the ivy behind the rose-filled flower pot.

sheaf, for example, makes an excellent accompaniment to a basket of autumn flowers, Chinese lanterns and peacock plant.

Sweetcorn, or maize, is a giant grass, and its outsized stalks, cobs still attached, can serve as a interesting seasonal support for large climbers such as kangaroo vine and grape ivy. A collection of house plants and adjacent container or containers of cut flowers can be combined into an autumnal display by winding long, leafless lengths of dried wild hops with their clusters of papery green seed heads, round and amongst the group. *Clematis vitalba*, with its feathery,

RIGHT The rich autumnal tones of coleus, *begonia rex* and eyelash begonia plants make an ideal backdrop for cut and dried sunflowers, dahlias and freshly-cut rosehips.

Plants

3 COLEUS
BEGONIA REX
EYELASH BEGONIA

Cut and Dried Flowers and Foliage

4-5 BRANCHES OF ROSEHIPS
4-5 BRANCHES OF WHITEBEAM
BERRIES
1 BUNCH OF DRIED SUNFLOWERS
1 BUNCH OF DRIED DAHLIAS
1 BUNCH OF DRIED, DYED BROOM
BLOOM
1 STEM OF GLYCERINED BEECH
LEAVES
2-5 PRESSED AND WIRED
JAPANESE MAPLE LEAVES

1 Place the coleus towards the back of a large tub. Place the begonias towards the front.
2 Pack the spaces between with dry florist's foam wedged to fit.
3 Insert the rosehips and whitebeam berries here and there to overhang the rim of the container. Infill with the dried sunflowers, dahlias, broom bloom and glycerined beech leaves. Finally, insert the Japanese maple leaves into any gaps in the arrangement.

whirlygig seed heads, makes a good alternative to wild hops.

Although combining fresh and dried flowers is often disappointing, since the fresh flowers make the dried ones look not merely dried but dead, combining dried grains and seedpods with fresh flowers is fine. Try combining poppy seed heads, bright orange lilies and the decorative foliage house plant angel wings.

❖

AUTUMN FOLIAGE

Deciduous tree and shrub foliage in autumnal colours is inevitably short lived in pot et fleurs. Nonetheless, for a special event, fresh autumn foliage in full blaze is worth the extra effort; delay cutting it for as long as possible and, if necessary, spray it with water to keep it turgid. With woody stems, dip the ends in boiling water for a few minutes, then give them a long cool drink.

Autumn leaves on long, flexible stems are especially valuable. Ornamental vines such as *Vitis vinifera* 'Purpurea', Virginia creeper or Boston ivy provide an excellent camouflage when wound round a plastic flower pot. They can also be trailed from a basket of house plants and cut flowers for an attractive table centrepiece.

Some mahonias, such as *Mahonia japonica*, produce a huge, flower-like rosette of radiating foliage at the tip of each stem. In autumn, when the foliage turns crimson, use one or more whole stems as the focal point of a large pot et fleur. Combine it with an umbrella tree or yucca and a few exotic cut blooms of painter's palette.

Autumn leaves can be used to good effect off the branch as well as on it. Set one or more house plants and a posy of autumnal flowers, such as sprays of Michaelmas daisies and goldenrods, in a large transparent glass bowl lined with colourful autumn leaves – the brilliant yellows of tulip trees; the red of various maples; the brown, yellow and green-veined horse chestnuts; or the brilliant orange-scarlet compound leaves of the stag's-horn sumach. Naturally dried bracken, ranging from beige to rich golden brown and copper, can serve as a decorative mat on which to build up a composite pot et fleur. If the bracken curls or arches, make use of these forms in the display.

RIGHT Chilli peppers, including those sold as house plants, can be red, yellow or green and range in fierceness from fairly to unbearably hot. Always handle them with care, since they can cause skin rashes – gloves are safest – and never rub your eyes after handling them. Cut branches of chilli peppers are shown here hanging, but they can also be inserted, right-way-up, into a wide range of house plants. The sea lavender air-dries naturally, so you can insert it into dry florist's foam or crumpled wire mesh.

Plants
2 CHRISTMAS PEPPERS
2 *EXACUM AFFINE*

Cut Flowers
1 LARGE BUNCH OF SEA LAVENDER

1 Place the Christmas peppers, still in their pots, in the centre of a large basket, alternating them.
2 Pack any remaining space in the basket with dry florist's foam.
3 Insert sea lavender sprigs evenly around the plants, to form a dense outer halo and fill any gaps in the centre.

If foliage such as elaeagnus, sweet chestnut, birch, fatsia and magnolia is preserved by replacing its water content with glycerine or antifreeze, it does not wilt or fade and remains flexible. The preserved foliage usually turns brown or beige, and is especially effective in pot et fleurs with coloured-leaved house plants. If you combine glycerined leaves with green house plant foliage, try to include flowers, fruits or seedpods in the orange/crimson/russet range, to act as a visual link between the two. Eucalyptus foliage is an exception, turning rich purple when fully glycerined, and purple-veined grey when partially glycerined. This makes it useful for a wide range of combinations.

❖

FRUITS AND VEGETABLES

Many edible fruits and vegetables are as attractive as purely ornamental ones; in terms of pot et fleur, the division is irrelevant. Sprigs of blackberries in berry, for example, especially the cut-leaved form, make a first-class filler for a straggly polka-dot plant or shrimp plant.

Use fruit colours and forms as the inspiration for autumnal compositions. In a large basket, mound purple-black figs, violet and white turnips, black grapes and blueberries around a large, purple-flowered gloxinia or a Cape primrose, with cut trailing stems of *Vitis vinifera* 'Purpurea' and branches of the purple-leaved Venetian sumach. House plant alternatives could include purple African violets, purple-leaved foliage plants such as wandering sailor, or the unusual, purple-tinged *Rhodochiton atrosanguineum*, now being sold as a 'patio plant' for hanging baskets.

If you grow your own courgettes, or zucchini, or have access to a pick-your-own farm, pick the courgettes with their flowers still attached. Impale them on florist's stub wires, then insert them either in the potting compost of a large-leafed finger plant, or in some florist's foam in a display with trailing nasturtiums and potted ferns such as brake fern.

At the end of the season, green tomatoes, especially long clusters

ABOVE AND LEFT The latter part of autumn forms the run-up to Christmas, with its red and green theme, and the cyclamen, eyelash begonia and *gaultheria* form the perfect basis for a festive pot et fleur, with apples adding a further 'transitional' touch. Part of the attractiveness is the close proximity of the plants, with leaves of one house plant overlapping the other, as if in nature. Freesias are widely available and delightfully scented but can look lonely on their own. Here, small bunches are inserted into the house plants to the benefit of all concerned. To achieve the maximum pleasure from the freesias, remove the spent lower florets and keep the display cool, out of direct sunlight and well watered.

of dwarf varieties, can make a witty component of pot et fleurs: drape them on the branches of a table-top weeping fig or jade tree.

Wild mushrooms can be obtained almost all year round in temperate climates, but are at their most plentiful in autumn. Collect bright orange chanterelles, variously coloured russulas and boletus, and re-erect them in a pot et fleur composed of mossy house plants such as moss fern or mind-your-own-business, rusty-orange cut chrysanthemums and a few autumn leaves or hazel nuts.

Plants
1 CYCLAMEN
1 EYELASH BEGONIA
2 *GAULTHERIA PROCUMBENS*

Cut Flowers and Foliage
1 LARGE BUNCH OF FREESIAS

1 Place the cyclamen, in its pot, at the back of the basket, the begonia at the front, and one gaultheria on each side. Pack the space between them with saturated florist's foam.
2 Cut the freesia stems so that they come to slightly above the height of the plants. Use florist's wire to tie them, fairly low down the stems, into small bunches.
3 Insert the freesias, here and there, in the florist's foam, angling some bunches outwards to overhang the rim.

ORNAMENTAL FRUIT

The fishbone cotoneaster, or wall spray, is almost too familiar as garden ground cover or a wall shrub for its autumnal beauty to be fully appreciated. Branches inserted in the centre of a mature asparagus fern create a horticultural pun on the fern's own rarely produced red berries – the 'fern' is actually a member of the lily family, and not a fern at all. If you want a floral element, add red florist's roses. Roses and asparagus ferns are a traditional florist's partnership, and the cotoneaster's vivid autumn leaves and berries give it character.

Many of the rowans and hawthorns also combine glorious berry and leaf colour, and can be used in a similar way. Rugosa roses, often grown as hedging for their dense, thorny growth, produce huge, bright orange apple-like hips, set in yellow autumn foliage. Use sprigs, in leaf or leafless, to enliven a painted drop tongue or button fern.

Euonymus europaeus, a native of British hedgerows, especially on chalky soils, produces heavy crops of orange berries in deep-pink outer capsules. Use the angled branches as a background for hot-pink Guernsey lilies and geranium house plants in bloom. The seedpods of some hypericums, such as *H.* x *inodorum* 'Elstead' are bright red, like miniature conical peppers. Use them with bright-pink dahlias, amaryllis and pink-flowered Madagascar periwinkle.

A few garden shrubs have almost too many berries to look natural, or berries so large in relation to the scale of the foliage or shrub itself that they look faintly ridiculous. Varieties of the South American ericaceous dwarf shrub *Pernettya mucronata* are prime examples. The artificiality of their marble-sized, white, pink, lilac or ruby-red berries can be turned to good advantage in pot et fleurs. Combine cut sprigs in berry with cyclamen and the curious purple autumnal blooms of *Liriope muscari*, or with hot-pink Guernsey lilies or seasonless Singapore orchids from the florist.

As winter approaches, ivy's green berries turn a subtle greybrown, and the mature, fruiting branches of so-called 'tree ivy' can be inserted in the compost of lax house plants such as wandering Jew, variegated buffalo grass or wandering sailor. You can use the ivy's

RIGHT Rosehips and cotoneaster berries, depending on the weather and the birds, can last well into autumn, even early winter. Branches can be cut in advance – even a week or two ahead – and kept in a bucket of water in a cool but frost-free spot.

Plants
1 CYCLAMEN
1 EYELASH BEGONIA
2 *GAULTHERIA PROCUMBENS*

Cut Foliage and Berries
COTONEASTER BRANCHES
ROSE BRANCHES
VIRGINIA CREEPER

1 Place the cyclamen, in its pot, at the back of the basket, the begonia at the front, and one gaultheria on each side. Pack the space between them with saturated florist's foam.
2 Cut the rose and cotoneaster branches into various lengths. Strip off any lower leaves and insert, here and there, in the florist's foam, angling some branches slightly downwards to overhang the basket rim.
3 Finally, at the last possible moment, loosely wrap long, leafy stems of Virginia creeper around the base of the basket.

erect, tree-like branches as a natural form of support, and gently manoeuvre a few of the longer stems upwards. Alternatively, angle them down and outwards to make a pretty ruffle round compact, autumn-flowering house plants such as Persian violets.

For an autumnal dish-garden with an unusual touch, wire up some ornamental dried bracket fungi (available from florist's shops) and to insert them in moss at the foot of, for example, the autumn-fruiting bread plant. For height and added colour, add some stinking iris seedpods with their brilliant orange berries.

❖

HARVEST DISPLAYS

A harvest display can use any autumnal material but some reference should be made to edible things. A simple suggestion is to fill a bowl or basket with whatever foliage house plants you have to hand, add a bunch of florist's flowers such as Peruvian lilies or gerberas in autumnal tones, a few branches of oak in autumn leaf, and then cover the surface of the potting compost with mixed nuts.

Edwardian harvest decorations often included animal as well as vegetable bounty: heaps of moss and heather, for example, with dozens of slain partridges tucked amongst the greenery, gracing the dining table. Although this is unlikely to appeal to modern sensibilities, flowers made out of pheasant tail feathers or pheasant, chicken or partridge breast feathers could be included in harvest pot et fleurs.

Wicker or wooden carved chickens or ducks, or even good quality plastic decoys, can sit in a 'nest' of dried grains or moss. Fill the cavity of a chicken- or duck-shaped wicker basket or a ceramic tureen with house plants and dried grasses, wired-up chestnuts and a small ornamental gourd or two.

A dried herb ring, decorated with herbs such as garlic, bayleaves, rosemary, artemisia, thyme and chillies can make a fragrant table decoration for a harvest supper. Place it horizontally in the middle of the table and fill the centre with a small pot chrysanthemum, concealing its plastic pot with a cachepot or plaited raffia.

As a buffet-table extravaganza, combine mixed ivies and fern house

plants with fresh or glycerined bells of Ireland, leek or ornamental onion seed heads, dried globe thistles, aubergines, apples, plums and cabbages with their outer leaves opened to form 'roses'. Mound the fruit and vegetables to conceal the flower pots and florist's foam. Harvest displays tend to look most convincing if home-grown or local fruits and vegetables are used. If they are slightly asymmetrical or imperfect, so much the better! Try to include old-fashioned produce such as quinces or medlars.

Cornucopias symbolise harvest bounty whether they are horn-shaped woven baskets or are created out of the harvest produce itself. Lay a wicker cornucopia on its side, and then fill it with hay or dried moss. Place miniature bromeliads such as earth stars or miniature ivies in the hay or moss so that their pots are concealed, and add pears, apples, figs and dried flowers. Alternatively, you could try filling a hollowed-out pumpkin with ivy or with a large rosette-forming bromeliad such as guzmania, wired-up kumquats or chestnuts, dried achillea, love-in-a-mist seedpods, Chinese lanterns and quaking grass. Or hollow out a cottage loaf and fill it with a mixture of tiny house plants and dried flowers.

LEFT These freshly cut Chinese lanterns are 'growing' in little flower pots filled with potting compost – a bit of poetic licence, and a pretty accompaniment to the more obviously cut sunflowers and wispy dried Chinese lanterns in the background.

Cut Flowers
5 SUNFLOWERS
3 CHINESE LANTERN STEMS

1 Insert saturated florist's foam into each flower pot, to come 2.5cm (1in) below the rim and wedge tightly.

2 Cut the Chinese lantern stems 8-10cm (3-4in) below the lowest lantern and insert individually into the florist's foam. Conceal the foam with a thick layer of potting compost.

3 Fill a container with water, and insert the sunflowers.

WINTER

❖ ❖ ❖

FLOWERS AND FOLIAGE ARE EVEN MORE IMPORTANT INDOORS WHEN THE GARDEN

IS DARK AND BARE, AND CHRISTMAS, WITH ITS WEALTH OF ORNAMENTATION AND

SYMBOLISM, IS AN ADDED INVITATION TO CREATIVITY.

❖ ❖ ❖

RIGHT Poinsettias and rex begonias make an unusual combination, visually and geographically – the former Mexican in origin, and the latter from Assam, in India. The third ingredient in this easy-to-make display is *Garrya elliptica*, a slightly tender, broad-leaved evergreen from California. Lastly, there is 'home-grown' ivy, as handsome as any exotic, especially when in berry. A subtle alternative would be to substitute a white or milky-pink poinsettia for the red variety.

Plants

POINSETTIA

BEGONIA REX

Cut Flowers and Foliage

4-6 SPRIGS OF *GARRYA ELLIPTICA*
4-6 SPRIGS OF TREE IVY IN BERRY

1 Place the poinsettia and rex begonia, still in their pots, in a basket or other outer container. Try to interweave the begonia leaves and flower-like poinsettia bracts.
2 Pack the spaces between with pieces of saturated florist's foam, wedged to fit tightly.
3 Insert the garrya and ivy to form a loose outer ruff. Angle some upwards, and others downwards, to conceal the rim.

Many long-term flowering house plants such as hibiscus and oleander are flowerless in winter and can benefit from 'borrowed' fresh cut, dried or silk flowers and fruit: silk cymbidiums or Singapore orchids rising from a rosette of *streptocarpus* leaves, for example, or silk lilacs framed by a vertical ring of hoya foliage. Long-term foliage house plants make good raw material for winter pot et fleurs: for example, you could use a few silk lilies to give a seasonal pick-me-up to an aspidistra.

❖

CHRISTMAS DISPLAYS

Christmas as a commercial enterprise begins well in advance of the event, so a good variety of cut conifer foliage is available from florists from mid-autumn. This can be used for dramatic pot et fleurs, or for adding a little visual weight to a modest house plant: creating a 'nest' of moss, conifer cones and cut conifer sprigs in a glass bowl, for example , for a single mini-cyclamen, miniature rose or African violet in flower. Inexpensive house plants are stocked in large numbers by high street chain stores and supermarkets for the Christmas gift market, so there is plenty of raw material for pot et fleurs to hand. Red, green, white and metallic tones, and holly, ivy, mistletoe and conifers are so strongly symbolic and emotive that a red ceramic bowl, moss and a few sprigs of mistletoe can instantly transform a small, white-flowered azalea, polyanthus or forced hyacinth into a Christmas pot et fleur.

Christmas is a good excuse to push back the frontiers of the visually extravagant. Any sculptural seed heads, from poppy and teazels to carthamus, artichoke, protea and acanthus, can be sprayed silver, gold, copper or bronze to add Christmas dazzle to dull house plants: tall, metallic-sprayed acanthus spikes, for example, 'growing' from the base of a Chinese fan palm or kentia palm.

Insert a mixture of metallic-sprayed seed heads, with varying stem lengths, into the top of a big, arching *Asparagus sprengeri*. Poppy seed heads, on their attenuated stems, are particularly attractive when used this way, creating the effect of cathedral-like spires. Metallic-

sprayed and wired-up pinecones can add a Christmassy feel to otherwise anonymous foliage house plants such as peperomias, creeping figs and holly ferns. Try combining metallic-sprayed lotus seedpods and metallic-sprayed dried hydrangea flower heads with a large rex begonia, or, for a more obvious Christmas theme, combine any of the above sprayed seedpods and house plants with bright red dried craspedia heads, or velvety red dried celosia.

Bamboo foliage quickly dries when cut, forming flag-like shapes. Insert tall, metallic-sprayed stems in the potting compost of a large Swiss cheese plant, or any of the larger philodendrons. The dried seedheads of *alliums* or ornamental onions and leeks are ideal for metallic spray-painting, and create the effect of firework explosions suspended in time – insert several, with different length stems, in the potting compost of an asparagus fern.

Poinsettias have been used as Christmas decorations for many years – the Victorians used them as cut flowers, first stemming the flow of milky sap by sealing the cut end with a match flame or boiling water. Today, poinsettias are sold only as house plants. Small poinsettias can look gawky on their own, so try filling a large jug with mixed twigs and foliage, and tuck the potted poinsettia in amongst the cut material, making sure its container is well hidden. This works equally well for small winter cherry plants, Christmas heather and Christmas pepper house plants and ornamental cabbages. If your funds allow, fill a big wicker basket or soup tureen with three or four large poinsettias, still in their pots, cut branches of variegated holly, variegated ivy and mistletoe and wired-up pinecones. Cover any visible potting compost or florist's foam with moss or Christmas-tree balls.

For a change from poinsettias, try putting small house plants such as brightly coloured kalanchoes, cyclamen, polyanthus or miniature roses in glass bowls filled with metallic-sprayed nuts or pebbles or fresh cranberries (in cool conditions, cranberries should last two weeks). Metallic-sprayed twigs or seedpods or cut sprigs of gypsophilla inserted amongst the plants will give the display vertical impact. For

LEFT In Georgian England pineapple stone finials on entrance gates and roofs, and pineapple plants grown in conservatories were the latest status symbol. Cut stalks of miniature pineapples are equally fashionable today.

Plants
5 POLYANTHUS

Cut Flowers and Fruit
3 MINIATURE PINEAPPLES
4-5 HYACINTHS
2 BUNCHES OF *NARCISSUS TAZETTA* 'SOLEIL D'OR' OR OTHER BUNCH-FLOWERED NARCISSI

1 Place the polyanthus, still in their pots, in the centre of a shallow basket or other container.
2 Pack the spaces between with pieces of saturated florist's foam, wedged to fit tightly.
3 If necessary, cut the pineapple stalks so that the fruits, when inserted, will sit just above the polyanthus. Insert the pineapples at even intervals and radiating out from the centre to form a triangle.
4 Cut the hyacinth stems and insert between the pineapples. Insert the narcissi in small bunches around the edge of the arrangement. Cover any visible florist's foam with damp moss.

LEFT AND RIGHT House plants with small ornamental fruits are ready-made starting points for pot et fleurs. Here, Christmas peppers and Christmas cherries provide a dome of greenery and 'baubles' of orange and yellow and traditional Christmas scarlet. You can also buy long cut branches of fresh ornamental peppers, or capsicums, which can be used as the cut-flower element of pot et fleurs, perhaps inserted in an out-of-flower cymbidium or clivia or ferns. In the arrangement opposite the flower-covered, wand-like stems of *Euphorbia fulgens* complement the round shapes of the Christmas fruits.

a dining-table centrepiece, lay a traditional Christmas wreath horizontally on the table, place one or more small house plants in the centre and pack the intervening space with moss. Or you could create a central 'fountain' of mistletoe, white Singapore orchids and green fatsia berries in a big basket and surround it with white African violets in flower.

Pomegranates are associated with Christmas and are relatively inexpensive at that time of year. Given a thin frosting of metallic paint, they become quite exotic. Impaled on dowels or sturdy branches, a cluster of pomegranates, possibly with some sprayed alliums, can 'grow' from a clivia, spathiphyllum or large brake fern. Alternatively, hang gold-frosted pomegranates from tree-like house plants such as weeping fig, umbrella tree, sparmannia, oleander, myrtle or citrus

Plants
CHRISTMAS PEPPER
3-5 CHRISTMAS CHERRIES

Cut Flowers
8-12 STEMS OF *EUPHORBIA
FULGENS*
SPHAGNUM MOSS

*1 Place the Christmas pepper,
still in its pot, in the centre of a
bowl or basket, and place the
Christmas cherries, in their pots,
in a tight circle around it.
2 Pack the spaces between the
pots with saturated florist's
foam. Insert the euphorbia
branches in the foam, radiating
out from the centre. Angle some
down over the rim, others
upwards.
3 Generously cover any
remaining surface with fresh
sphagnum moss.*

trees. Tree-like plants such as jade trees, which are too small to bear the weight of pomegranates, can sport gold-sprayed and wired-up walnut 'fruits'.

Christmas 'multiples' – clusters of plant- and flower-filled containers displayed close together – can look very festive. It helps if the containers are identical or similar: metallic-sprayed terracotta flower pots, for example, or identical deep red or blue glass tumblers. Pack some containers with saturated florist's foam and fill them with one type of seasonal cut flower or foliage such as mistletoe, holly, tree ivy, chincherinchees or gold-sprayed pine cones. Alternate these with containers of mind-your-own-business. More simply, display a cluster of mind-your-own business house plants – some with tiny 'trees' of gold-sprayed alder twigs inserted – interspersed with simple glass tumblers, each filled with a single anemone or gerbera.

RIGHT HERE, solidago, or goldenrod, makes an airy contribution to the solid silhouette of the Christmas pepper and cherries. A jug filled with hypericum in berry and orange carthamnus thistles repeats the red, orange and green theme.

Plants
CHRISTMAS PEPPER
3-5 CHRISTMAS CHERRIES

Cut Flowers
8-10 STEMS OF SOLIDAGO

1 Place the Christmas pepper, still in its pot, in the centre of a bowl or basket, and place the Christmas cherries, in their pots, in a tight circle around it.
2 Pack the spaces between the pots with saturated florist's foam. Cut the solidago stems so that they will hover above the plants, then insert them, radiating out from the centre, in the florist's foam. Angle some down over the rim, others upwards.

In a big basket or bowl, cluster leafy house plants round a central tumbler of water filled with 'Paperwhite' narcissi, chincherinchees, brightly coloured anemones or Turk's-cap ranunculus. Pack the space between the pots with damp peat and top with moss, to create a continuous green surface. As the flowers fade, you can replace them with fresh ones. For an especially fragrant centrepiece, include cut sprigs of wintersweet, winter-flowering honeysuckle, winter box or daphne from the garden.

Candles added to house plant and cut-flower displays can give a festive look, but care should always be taken to ensure that they are stable before lighting. Tall candles can be inserted directly into the potting compost of low-growing house plants. As a multiple display, arrange a cluster or straight line of whisky tumblers, each containing a different element – for example, tiny house plants, tightly-packed mistletoe, roses or chrysanthemums, or candles.

Raised cake or ham stands are in great demand at Christmas but if you have one to spare, use it as the basis for a pot et fleur featuring small-leafed trailing house plants such as ivy, tradescantias, trailing sedums or peperomias, along with candles, mistletoe, chincherinchee and metallic-sprayed Peking willow impaled on a central block of florist's foam.

There is life after Christmas, and perhaps even more need for cheerful pot et fleurs as the bills come in and January temperatures dip. Post-Christmas prices dip, too, and many house plants, cut flowers and silk flowers are much reduced. The January sales are a good opportunity to stock up with these, and with glass baubles and other Christmas tree ornaments, artificial fruits, tiny birds, candles and candleholders, ribbons and pretty boxes, to be stored away and used for next Christmas' pot et fleurs.

❖

DWARF CONIFERS AND CONIFER FOLIAGE
Dwarf conifers are not house plants and dislike centrally heated conditions. They are, however, on the scale of house plants and can be used for temporary festive displays. Placed in a large cachepot

and surrounded with moss, a dwarf juniper, fir, spruce or thuja can become, for one night, a table-top Christmas tree decorated with tiny ribbons and balls and set in a hazy ring of cut gypsophila and glass Christmas-tree balls. Alternatively, a dwarf conifer could be included in a mixed house plant and cut-flower basket: one very attractive combination is a dwarf conifer, kalanchoes, moss and berried holly branches which have been stripped of their leaves.

A winter pot et fleur can provide the setting for a Nativity or other Christmas scene. Set dwarf conifers in a wooden box deep enough to conceal the containers, add cut twigs such as hazel or contorted willow and then pack the spaces between with peat and top with moss or sand. Alternatively, create the trees out of conifer branches and, as the house plant element of the pot et fleur display, include moss-like selaginellas, or cacti and succulents such as partridge-breasted aloe, lace aloe or pincushion cactus. You can then add your choice of Christmas figures – either a Nativity or a secular scene with Father Christmas and reindeer.

Cut branches of conifer range from the enormous – if you cut them yourself from the garden – to small sprays of less than 30cm long, but all are useful. Using red, white or metallic ribbons, tie a dense layer of evenly cut branches of blue fir, spruce, cedar or other flat-sprayed conifer around a flowerpot containing a poinsettia or lily, to create a pot et fleur cachepot with a Christmassy feel. Allow the branches to extend irregularly above the rim. This treatment is especially effective with pot chrysanthemums, as the conifer can conceal the chrysanthemum's own dull foliage. Alternatively, line a wire lettuce shaker with overlapping conifer sprigs and moss if wished, as a cachepot for a poinsettia, azalea or potted lily. Allow some of the conifer foliage to extend through the wires for a natural, nest-like effect.

A single, carefully selected old pine branch can have the beauty of a bonsai tree; insert one in a flowerpot or bulb bowl filled with forced mini-daffodils, crocus or snowdrops, and cover the potting compost with moss. As with all conifers indoors, cool temperatures and regular spraying with water will extend its display life.

ABOVE Here, *Kalanchoe blossfeldiana* is given a woodland setting far removed from its Madagascan origins. Leaves and cones have been glued to the candle holders.

Plants
2 OR 3 KALANCHOES
3 MIND-YOUR-OWN BUSINESS PLANTS

Cut Flowers
BUNCH OF BUPLEURUM

1 Place the kalanchoe in the centre of a basket or other container, raising it slightly so that the plants sit above the rim.
2 Place the mind-your-own-business plants at even intervals around the kalanchoe. Pack any spaces with saturated florist's foam.
3 Cut sprigs of bupleurum and insert dense bunches between the mind-your-own-business plants.

RIGHT Nothing could be simpler than inserting a few sinuous branches of contorted willow (also called curly, twisted or Peking willow) into a cyclamen. The willow branches can be as tall and as wide-spreading as the base will support, and visually command a significantly larger area than the house plant.

Plants
CYCLAMEN

Cut Branches and Fruit
LARGE BRANCH OF CONTORTED WILLOW
3 POMEGRANATES

1 Place the cyclamen, still in its pot, in a basket or similar container.
2 Cut the contorted willow to the required lengths and insert them in the potting compost.

Many conifers that are ideal for pot et fleurs are not available commercially as cut foliage. If you have the space, it is worth building up a collection of larger conifers for use as year-round raw material. Branches of junipers or yews with horizontal growth habits can create a miniature landscape when displayed with a small flowering azalea and a surface finish of gravel or moss. Cryptomerias are airier, lacier and less linear in the growth habit of their foliage than most other conifers and varieties that turn russet red in winter are

105

especially valuable. Combine cut sprays with gerberas, arching sprays of *Euphorbia fulgens* and a purple-tinged philodendron, such as the variety 'Burgundy', *P. erubescens,* or the peacock plant *Calathea makoyana.*

Buddhist pine is occasionally grown as a house plant and its elegant, glossy, long, leaf-like needles make an excellent component for a pot et fleur with virtually any cut flower. Cut foliage from garden species, such as *Podocarpus salignus,* is equally useful; combine either with cut or potted lilies, gerberas and leafless larch branches.

❖

BROAD-LEAVED EVERGREENS

These year-round stalwarts are especially valuable in winter, when deciduous plants are leafless. For an instant pot et fleur, fill a huge vase or jug with cut evergreen foliage such as bay, box, elaeagnus, evergreen oak, camellia, pittosporum, aucuba, eucalyptus, arbutus, Mexican orange or pieris, and tuck in a small, colourful house plant such as a fairy primrose or Christmas pepper, angled as if growing from the centre of the vase. Use trailing stems of ivy to break the line of the vase rim and, if necessary, camouflage the flowerpot.

Variegated broad-leaved evergreens have additional advantages. Those with green and white variegations – varieties of holly, ivy, box, euonymus, cotoneaster and even pachysandra (sometimes classed as a perennial) – are Christmassy by their very nature. Inserting lanky, pendant branches of white-variegated holly directly in the potting compost of an old, specimen Christmas cactus not only counteracts the oddly angular growth habit that Christmas cacti often have, but at the same time adds a distinctly festive note. You can do the same thing with other arching house plants such as the emerald fern *Asparagus densiflorus* 'Sprengeri' or the unusual miniature wax plant, *Hoya bella*.

Some broad-leaved evergreens such as skimmia, aucuba, holly and cotoneaster come with the benefit of berries, according to the whim of birds and weather; these can add extra colour to pot et fleurs.

ABOVE AND RIGHT Unless they are substantial, azaleas can get lost in the general visual mêlée at Christmas-time. Here, three azaleas in a basket form the foundation for an attractive pot et fleur; grouping same-colour azaleas, or indeed any variety of house plant in flower, has a more unified effect than grouping mixed flower colours. Variegated *Pittosporum tobira* and artificial berries are shown, but holly branches in berry, stripped of their leaves, and variegated evergreen euonymus could be substituted.

Plants
3 AZALEAS

Berries and Foliage
8-10 SPRIGS OF VARIEGATED
PITTOSPORUM
6 STEMS OF ARTIFICIAL BERRIES

1 Place the azaleas, still in their pots, in a basket or other container.
2 Pack the spaces between the pots with saturated florist's foam. Cut the pittosporum to extend slightly above the azaleas and insert the sprigs in the foam, radiating out from the centre.
3 Insert tall stems of artificial berries, again radiating out from an imaginary central point.

Interestingly, certain berrying shrubs take on a more sophisticated appearance if stripped of their leaves. The green, then red, berries of aucuba are visually overwhelmed by their outsized, yellow splashed leaves, awkward to use in all but the largest flower arrangements. With the foliage removed, the green, berry-laden stems become less dominant and much more versatile. Holly branches in berry take on an entirely different character with their foliage removed; holly berries are produced on year-old wood, so it is sensible to trim back any bare stem beyond the berries.

Various hebes may have their flowers intact into winter, or even until Christmas if the winter is mild. Though not essentially

Christmassy, branches of hebe in flower – purple, blue and fuchsia pink – can be combined with the fuchsia-pink of Christmas cacti or azalea house plants in bloom.

Larger-growing mahonias such as *M. japonica* and *M.* 'Charity' have a fountain-like growth habit, with dramatic rosettes of evergreen pinnate leaves on vertical stems, topped in winter with scented racemes of yellow blooms. Again, not a traditional Christmas colour, but two or three stems, 30-45cm (12-18in) long, can be inserted in the potting compost of a lanky fatsia, Swiss cheese plant, umbrella tree or dumb cane. If they escape weather damage, the pale-green hanging catkins of *Garrya elliptica* can add an appealing softness to a pot et fleur of Christmas pepper house plants and cut stems of winter-flowering jasmine, witch hazel and laurustinus in flower.

Pittosporum branches often subdivide neatly, like a small tree. Set out a row of winter-flowering polyanthus or other small flowering house plants in a rectangular container packed with potting compost and topped with moss, then insert a row of pittosporum branches behind, as a linear landscape. Alternatively, place a forest of pittosporum branches in the centre of a circular container, and surround it with an outer circle of flowering house plants.

Forced hyacinths and narcissi are popular Christmas house plants and are also available as cut flowers. Combine cut and growing hyacinths, hippeastrums or narcissi in a pot et fleur, the cut blooms in a simple glass tumbler with cut pittosporum, some tall twigs of pittosporum inserted in the bulb potting compost, and perhaps a tumbler or two of pittosporum on its own.

Like pittosporum, mature, berrying branches of ivy are structured like diminutive trees. They can last for a week or more out of water, and can be inserted in the potting compost of leggy house plants such as cane begonias or yuccas. Tree ivy can also be arranged as a nest in which one or more small house plants sit; arrange a row of small house plants and one or more container of cut flowers on a fireplace mantelpiece or shelf, then intertwine tree ivy between and among the various containers, to create a solid mass.

LEFT Old-fashioned florist's asparagus fern is traditionally associated with bunches of long-stemmed roses, but here it creates a delicate, airy outline to this simple pot et fleur of cut lilies rising above potted azaleas.

Plants
3 AZALEAS

Cut Flowers and Foliage
3-5 LILY STEMS
10-12 FRONDS OF ASPARAGUS FERN

1 Place the azaleas, still in their pots, in a basket or other container.
2 Pack the spaces between the pots with saturated florist's foam, ensuring that there is a substantial block in the centre. Cut the lily stems to extend well above the azaleas and insert them close together in the central block to form a fountain-like effect.
3 Insert the asparagus fern to form a low, wide-spreading ruffle round the base.

Many broad-leaved evergreens that are today considered garden plants – aucuba, box, camellia, euonymus, eucalyptus, myrtle and fatsia – are listed in some older gardening books as house plants. They do need masses of ventilation and cool temperatures to survive indoors but plants in containers, including charming micro-standard box trees on 10cm (4in) stems, can be combined with cut flowers for a few days indoors.

Camellias are grown for their flowers but have handsome, glossy leaves. Young plants, barely more than a single, 30cm (12in) high stem, are often sold in winter, laden with bloom. Use them as a temporary plant component of a pot et fleur, perhaps with holly ferns, Peking

ABOVE AND LEFT African violets can be found in flower all year round, with pale yellow as the latest addition to a wide colour range. Bouvardias need frequent re-cutting to ensure that there is a continuous supply of water to the blooms; removing the leaves helps extend their display life.

Plants
3 AFRICAN VIOLETS

Cut Flowers and Foliage
5 STEMS OF BOUVARDIA
4 STEMS OF SMILAX

1 Place the African violets in a basket or other container.
2 Pack the spaces between with saturated florist's foam.
3 Cut the bouvardia stems to come flush with the African violets and insert amongst the African violet foliage. Insert smilax around the edge.

RIGHT Statice is particularly useful fot pot et fleurs because it comes in a wide range of colours from pastel to vibrant and retains its fresh colour when dried. You can also use freshly cut statice in pot et fleurs, where it will dry of its own accord. Here, pale pink statice is combined with African violets. Broidaea is added for a touch of blue.

Plants
3 AFRICAN VIOLETS

Cut Flowers and Foliage
1 BUNCH OF PINK STATICE
12-15 STEMS OF BRODIAEA

1 Place the African violets, still in their pots, in a basket or other container.
2 Pack the spaces between with saturated florist's foam.
3 Cut the statice stems to come flush with the African violets and insert in tight clumps amongst the African violet foliage. Insert brodiaea stems around the edge.

willow and moss – all components with Oriental origins or overtones. If you have the luxury of cutting large camellia branches in bloom from an established camellia, insert them in the base of a large Chinese fan palm.

Finally, using a house plant as the base, you can create a luxurious-looking standard, half-standard or mini-standard topiary with cut box or conifer foliage. Roughly shape one-third to one-half of a block of saturated florist's foam to form a globe and impale it on a dowel or sturdy tree branch. Insert the other end in the potting compost of a low-growing house plant such as eyelash begonia or variegated buffalo grass, *Stenotaphrum secundatum* 'Variegatum'.

(A terracotta flowerpot will help stabilise the display better than a light-weight plastic one.) Insert sprigs of box or other small-leafed evergreen or conifer in the globe until it is densely packed and completely covered. Add cut flowers such as gypsophila or baby rosebuds as required.

❖

COLOURED BARK AND BRANCHES

In cool temperate climates, red- and yellow-barked dogwood are probably the most common coloured-bark shrubs and are worth growing for their garden value alone. The coral-barked *Acer palmatum* 'Senkaki', however lovely, is so slow growing that substantial pruning for pot et fleur material is out of the question. There are also varieties of willow with red, yellow and purple bark but, even stooled, they grow too large for the average garden. Unfortunately, none of these is available commercially, but you are able to buy leafless branches of twisted Peking willow, which has become something of a 'designer accessory' for flower arrangers. From woodland and hedgerow you can gather leafless branches of hazel with its pretty catkins, and alder with its oriental-looking cones.

Leafless dormant branches with coloured bark or an attractive growth habit need no water, and can be treated like dried or silk material. For high drama, insert tall stems or branches, 1m or more high, in the potting compost of a house plant or in the florist's foam of a composite pot et fleur. If you have out-of-flower cymbidium orchids, for example, try inserting big stems of twisted willow behind the orchid foliage. Then add cut cymbidiums or other orchids, either fresh or silk, as if the orchids were growing on a tree trunk as in their natural habitat.

Alternatively, you can go for 'designer stubble', by cutting the branches to identical short lengths, rather like bristles of a broom. In late winter, try potting up a clump of snowdrops or winter-flowering iris in bud or early blossom and then cover the potting compost with moss. To one side insert a cluster of short-stemmed, picturesque branches cut to an identical height.

LEFT Here, pink miniature rose house plants, available all year round, are combined with silvery kochia. The styling of pot et fleurs can extend to include nearby ornaments; here, pewter jugs, mugs and candlesticks, some filled with fragrant pink bouvardia, create a clustered focal point.

Plants
3 MINIATURE ROSES

Cut Flowers and Foliage
5 STEMS OF KOCHIA
4-5 STEMS OF BOUVARDIA

1 Insert the roses, still in their pots, in a pewter bowl or similar container.
2 Pack the spaces between the rose pots and the container with pieces of saturated florist's foam, wedged to fit tightly.
3 Cut the stems of kochia so that the top of the foliage shows above the roses. Insert them around the rose pots, radiating outwards from an imaginary central point.
4 Cut the bouvardia stems so that when inserted in two or more small containers the flower heads come just above the rims.

RIGHT *Jasminum polyanthum* is the most common jasmine house plant and blooms in late autumn and winter. Here, a small, hoop-trained specimen is combined with elegant, gold-sprayed seed heads, shells, nuts and oak leaves. One candle holder features gold-sprayed clam and scallop shells glued, petal-like, to the holder and interspersed with a 'necklace' of gold-sprayed larch cones.

Plants
HOOP-TRAINED JASMINE

Dried Material
8-12 GOLD-SPRAYED WALNUTS
6-8 GOLD-SPRAYED LEAVES
BUNCH OF GOLD-SPRAYED POPPY
SEED HEADS

1 Place the jasmine in a metallic or glass bowl. Fill the bowl with gold-sprayed walnuts and leaves. 2 Tie the poppies with a ribbon and place to one side. Complete by scattering a few of the walnuts.

Use cut branches with character, such as old, lichen-encrusted larch, to form supports for climbers such as stephanotis and hoya, perhaps adding silk flowers such as Turks'-cap ranunculus at the base. A lily or hippeastrum house plant in flower combines well with some lichen-covered larch and blue spruce branches. Bury the flower pot and the ends of the branches in water-washed pebbles in an old glass battery tank; all the ingredients should be tall enough to extend above the rim of the tank.

Branches of the female stag's-horn sumach have velvety clusters of hairy fruits at the tips, and if you can reach them, they can be used to great effect to support climbers or as a component in a more ambitious pot et fleur – say, with hellebores and a large, sprawling prayer plant or purple-tinged begonia. Cut branches can also add visual weight to a modest house plant. If you have a single African violet, mini-cyclamen or polyanthus in flower, try placing it, off centre, in a broad, shallow cachepot packed with damp peat and topped with moss. Add a few pebbles at the base of the plant, then insert several large, interestingly shaped branches, such as contorted hazel, to form a halo radiating outwards from the house plant.

❖

DRIED AND SILK MATERIAL

Good quality silk flowers are so lifelike in appearance that objections to their use can only be philosophical. Silk flowers can be inserted directly in potting compost and remain there indefinitely. You can use full-blown, old-fashioned summer lilacs or roses in defiance of the natural winter season, or stick to seasonal silk flowers such as poinsettias, azaleas, or 'forced' hyacinths or narcissi. Half a dozen good quality silk poinsettias or red or white silk anthuriums can 'grow' from a Buddhist pine, umbrella plant, grape ivy or kangaroo vine, with metallic-sprayed birch or hazel branches as an optional third element.

Silk flower stems and foliage are often disappointing, and it is best to conceal them with fresh house plant foliage: for example, silk lilies or iris can emerge from the strap-shaped leaves of a specimen-sized clivia. For instant sophistication, combine silk lilies, peonies or orchids with a specimen size stag's-horn fern or fan palm. For modest charm, combine silk tulips with a bird's-nest or Boston fern.

You can buy good quality fake conifer garlands of the type which are frequently used in American homes at Christmas time to decorate stair railings and fireplaces. They are very useful for concealing unattractive plastic flower pots, and for additional decoration, you can weave in twigs sprayed with metallic paint to extend above the rim of the pot.

Index of English and Latin Names

INDEX